DATE DUE

DEMCO 38-296

LANDS and PEOPLES

SPECIAL EDITION:
THE CHANGING FACE
OF EUROPE

GROLIER

LANDS and PEOPLES

SPECIAL EDITION:
THE CHANGING FACE
OF EUROPE

STAFF

Lawrence T. Lorimer . . . . . . .Editorial Director
Joseph M. Castagno . . . . .Editor in Chief
Laura Alsdorf . . . . .Editor
Doris E. Lechner . . . . .Director, Annuals
Irina Rybacek . . . . .Text Author
Jean Zambelli . . . . .Art Director
Meghan O'Reilly . . . . .Copy Editor
Jone E. Baltzell . . . . .Editorial Assistant
Karen A. Fairchild . . . . . .Editorial Assistant
Kenneth W. Leish . . . . .Managing Editor
Lisa J. Grize . . . . .Chief Photo Editor
Elissa G. Spiro . . . . .Photo Researcher
Elizabeth M. See . . .Assistant Photo Researcher
Jane H. Carruth . . . . .Manager, Picture Library
Anne Kugielsky . . . . . . .Production Editor
Pauline M. Sholtys . . . . .Chief Indexer
Linda King . . . . .Indexer
Joseph J. Corlett . .Vice President, Manufacturing
Christine L. Matta . . . . .Director of Reference
                    Publishing, Manufacturing
Rose V. DeMarco . . . . . .Production Manager
Ranjan Bhatt . . . . .Production Assistant

ISBN 0-7172-8019-5

On the cover: The flags of member countries fly in front of the European Union headquarters building in Brussels, Belgium.

Contents

Substantial strides have been made toward developing a sense of economic unity in Europe. Less progress has been made toward generating a unified European response to local crises.

The Changing Face of Europe

In Europe's long, turbulent history, the century that is now coming to a close has been possibly the most dramatic. In 1900, there were no automobiles, no television, no airplanes. Europe was the center of the world. The colonial empires of Britain and France reached across the globe. Unified Germany was only 30 years old, and had only begun to flex its muscle. Three large multinational empires—the Russian, the Austro-Hungarian, and the Ottoman empires—were entering the last years of their existence. The word "genocide" was unknown, as were the expressions "concentration camp," "totalitarianism," and "nuclear power."

The term "Communism," however, was already being used by small circles of revolutionaries throughout Europe, although not until 1917, when the Communist social experiment started in Russia, would most people know what the word meant. Before long, millions of people knew exactly what Communism stood for. When future historians write about the 20th century, they will discuss Communism and its impact as one of the era's chief characteristics.

This book offers a multilayered portrayal of Communism, concentrating on its disintegration, but also discussing its roots and its legacies. The introduction will begin with a look at the origins of the Communist movement, the main characteristics of Communist regimes, and daily life in Communist societies. It will also touch on the impact of Communism in the West, compare Communism with Nazism, and sum up recent developments. Next will come a section titled "Former Yugoslavia and Other Battlefields," which will deal with the bloody conflicts that have plagued those regions. The introduction will conclude with a section titled "European Integration."

After that comes the Chronology, which traces developments in the Communist world from 1944 onward. Events since 1992 are presented in two spreads: one for central Europe and the Balkans, the other for the republics of the former Soviet Union.

The names and terms that appear in boldfaced type in the Chronology are the main entries in the next major part of the book, the Alphabetical Overview, which consists of 121 short articles. The topics cover all the former Communist countries and the newly constituted successor states, some important regions, significant personalities, and various terms and organizations. These brief entries should serve as an orientation only. A more detailed treatment of individual countries appears in the main volumes of the **LANDS and PEOPLES** set.

The concluding section, "Looking Toward the Next Century," surveys the main problems that arose after the fall of Communist governments and considers the likely future developments in different regions.

In late 1995, American troops, as part of a NATO mission, were deployed to Bosnia in order to help enforce the peace accords signed by the warring factions.

The collapse of Communism and the dissolution of the Soviet Union led to the emergence of an independent Russia. Above, Muscovites unfurl the tricolor flag of pre-Communist days.

The Rise and Fall of Communism

Communist regimes have caused so much suffering in so many parts of the world that all other tyrannies throughout history pale in comparison. Ironically, this great modern tragedy started with a vision of a new and better world. Regardless of whether Marx, Lenin, and the other founding fathers of Communism were idealistic visionaries or ruthless power seekers, millions of people actually believed, some for a short time and others for their whole lives, that socialism and Communism were the noblest goals of human history.

In the mid-19th century, the German thinker Karl Marx formulated a theory of Communism as the highest stage in history, in which all exploitation and poverty would be abolished, all work would become creative, and the state with its powers of repression would vanish. Marx then "scientifically" predicted a world revolution that would usher in socialism, a transitory stage between capitalism and Communism. The rulers in this period would no longer be the "bourgeois" classes, but rather the working people, or proletariat, who would also own all means of production.

When the Russian revolutionary Vladimir Ilich Lenin formed his Bolshevik Party in 1905 (which was renamed "Communist" in 1917), he complemented the original Marxist vision with an important addition: in his view, the party would be the "vanguard of the proletariat." Lenin died

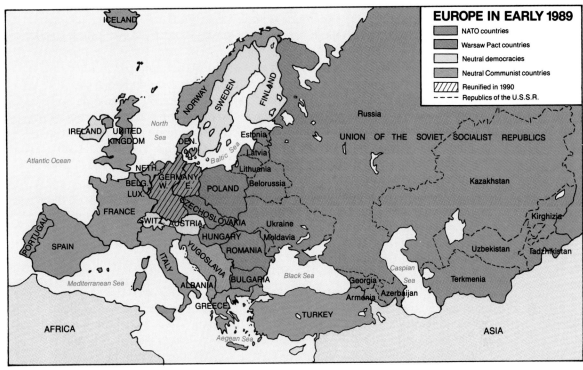

EUROPE IN EARLY 1989

- NATO countries
- Warsaw Pact countries
- Neutral democracies
- Neutral Communist countries
- Reunified in 1990
- Republics of the U.S.S.R.

After World War II, most of Eastern Europe came under Soviet domination. For almost 45 years, the continent was essentially split between a democratic west and a totalitarian east. National borders remained virtually unchanged throughout the period.

By early 1996, Europe looked considerably different. After the Soviet Union collapsed, the Commonwealth of Independent States (CIS) was formed to maintain ties among some former Soviet republics. The former Yugoslavia was torn apart by civil war.

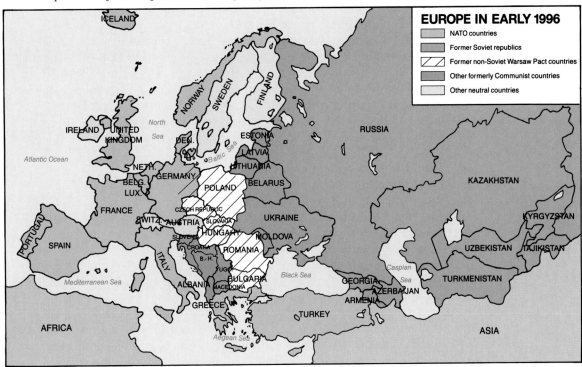

EUROPE IN EARLY 1996

- NATO countries
- Former Soviet republics
- Former non-Soviet Warsaw Pact countries
- Other formerly Communist countries
- Other neutral countries

several years after the Communists took over; students of Soviet history continue to ponder whether the Soviet regime would have become more benevolent had Lenin lived longer. Be that as it may, Lenin's successor was a seemingly colorless bureaucrat named Stalin, who in less than a decade became the supreme dictator of the Soviet Union. The system he created—Stalinism—resulted from a complex mixture of his own personality and Russian history and society: on the one hand, Stalin was manipulative, ruthless, ambitious, and, in his later years, quite paranoid; on the other hand, Russia had a history of autocracy and a population consisting mostly of illiterate peasants who equated the terms "democracy" and "freedom" with "anarchy."

At an almost unimaginable cost in human lives and suffering, Stalin transformed the Soviet Union from a feudal backward empire into an industrialized giant. Attacked by Nazi Germany in 1941, the country bore the heaviest brunt of World War II in the number of people killed and in physical destruction. The defeat of Hitler was in large part due to the Soviet Army.

In the closing months of the war, Soviet troops advanced west in pursuit of Germans, and their presence in central Europe and the Balkans helped set up "satellite" Communist regimes. Two exceptions were Yugoslavia and Albania, where strong national leaders appeared during the war: Josip Broz Tito and Enver Hoxha were both guerrilla heroes.

The first period of Communism in Eastern Europe was a somewhat diluted copy of the Stalinist 1930s: expropriation of private property, collectivization of agriculture, abolition of civil liberties, purges of anti-Communist opposition, persecution of "class enemies," show trials, executions, and widespread terror. After these years, Eastern Europe settled into a more lenient stage, less explicitly brutal, but in many ways more pernicious.

Meanwhile, Communist regimes arose in Asia. The second-oldest Communist country in the world, Mongolia, became a "People's Republic" in November 1924. After World War II, China and North Korea joined the Communist world, and, in 1954, North Vietnam followed suit. In 1959, Cuba set out on its Communist adventure. During the next decade, many African governments turned to Marxism. In the 1960s, with Communists controlling the largest country in the world (Soviet Union), the most populous country (China), and scores of smaller nations, it seemed that Communism was indeed marching toward victory.

The Main Characteristics of Communist Societies

The Leading Role of the Party. All ruling Communist parties had a constitutional monopoly on power. The first rule in George Orwell's *Animal Farm*, "All animals are equal, but some are more equal," precisely describes the situation. From top to bottom of society, party members in the Communist countries were more equal than others: they made decisions about everything—from the correct "party line" concerning some far-away regional conflict to the handling of young people with unconventional hairdos or a love for Western music.

The party and the state were intertwined, but the party was decisive. In several European countries, there were small subservient political parties, but they were just "window dressing" in the game of democracy. Another element in this "let's pretend" game was the ritual of elections.

For decades, Communist government bodies simply rubber-stamped the decisions of the party elite. A strong personality cult developed around the early leaders of the Communist era.

These regular happenings were, of course, not true elections: for each position, the party nominated one candidate only. Every citizen had to participate and the results were always just below 100 percent. The "elections" were supposed to show that the ruling Communist party enjoyed the full support of the people.

The persons occupying the high party and state positions were collectively known as the *nomenclature*. A crucial segment of the nomenclature was the secret police—in the Soviet Union, it was known by the acronym KGB; in East Germany, its name was *Stasi*. There were differences between individual countries. The secret police had an almost total grip on society in Albania and Romania, while in Hungary and Poland, they were less powerful. Tens of thousands of people helped the police as informers.

Not all party members believed in Communism, however. Particularly in the latter stages of Communism, many people joined the party for professional reasons, in order to advance their careers. Indeed, without a party card, it was virtually impossible to attain any high position.

The Ruling Ideology of Marxism-Leninism. Early in the Communist era, Marxism-Leninism was professed with a religious fervor by many people. A believing Communist often resembled a member of a dogmatic sect who always counters your objections with a ready argument. Over the years, however, Marxism-Leninism turned into a hollow incantation of phrases, a set of formulas and pronouncements. "All history until the advent of socialism was marked by class struggle between the oppressors and the oppressed," was one such formula; others ranged from a condemnation of profit-making as antisocial to the adulation of the Soviet Union as the "cradle of socialism." By being endlessly repeated, these "truths" were at least partially accepted by a great number of people. The brainwashing varied according to the time and the country—it gradually became quite perfunctory in Poland and in Hungary; in the hard-line regimes, such as Albania, Romania, and Bulgaria, no one dared to challenge it.

Communist countries tended to concentrate their resources on heavy industry. Much of this industry is now either obsolete or in need of revamping to make quality products for a world marketplace.

Censorship was the key tool used by the party to maintain its position. Anything published or publicly presented had to be approved by censors, but the state also relied on self-censorship: most citizens of the Communists societies quickly learned, out of an instinct for self-preservation, to be careful in what they said outside their closest circles of friends and family. All copying machines were strictly under state control; in Romania, even typewriters had to be registered.

Command Economy, the centrally planned economies of Marxist countries, was for decades hailed as the true "scientific" way to direct the economic life of a society. It had several basic characteristics:

• *Central Planning:* Economic decisions (what to produce, how to produce) were made by huge bureaucracies. Individual entrepreneurship, initiative, and industriousness were not only unwelcome, but were often punished by demotion or harassment.

• *Price Controls:* All prices were set by state agencies and often remained unchanged for years. Basic commodities and rents for apartments were heavily subsidized and thus very low.

• *State as the Major Employer:* The state sector was by far the largest employer (in some countries the only one); most or all people were therefore state employees. There was no unemployment. Uniformly low salaries provided little incentive to work hard, and a typical employee worked as little as possible.

• *Emphasis on Heavy Industry:* This went back to Stalin and his emphasis on huge industrial complexes. Czechoslovakia, for instance, produced a ton of steel for each inhabitant. Most of the Communist-built mammoth enterprises were rather inefficient.

• *Neglect of Services and Chronic Shortages:* Not only were there not enough stores, repair shops, restaurants, and other services, but the existing ones were poorly supplied. In 1988, for instance, the Soviet Union had 20 shops per 10,000 inhabitants, while Italy had 175.

• *Undeveloped Banking and Financial System:* Virtually everything was paid for in cash: salaries, wages, and all purchases. Checking accounts and credit cards did not exist; to buy on an installment plan was an exception rather than rule.

• *"Shadow Economy" and Black Market:* These complemented the malfunctioning official economic system. Because it was so difficult to obtain goods and services, there was a widespread barter economy and a network of connections: someone fixed your broken TV set, and you in return supplied him or her with black-market hard currency; another person got you a high-quality cut of beef, and you repaid with a bottle of Western perfume.

Daily Life in Communist Societies

After the initial times of terror, the majority of Communist countries settled into relative calmness. Most people had several basic certainties. They knew that unless they provoked the authorities with some political protest or even indiscretion, they would never lose their jobs. They knew that the basic foodstuffs would cost the same for years to come. They knew that they would get free education and free medical care, even if of low quality. They could also count on retirement pensions at a relatively early age, most often at the age of 55 for women and 60 for men.

The other certainties were the daily frustrations: standing endlessly in lines to get basics like food and clothing, arguing with grumpy salespeople, and trying not to fall into gaping street excavations that stayed unfinished for months. Electricity was often shut off and almost nothing seemed to function properly.

At work, unreliability and inefficiency were pervasive: nonworking telephones, delays in deliveries, nonsensical orders from above. At the same time, it was considered quite normal to go shopping during working hours or to the hairdresser—and to steal. It was said that "whoever does not steal from the state, steals from his family." Ironically, some passages in Marx's writing that describe working conditions in the glorious future of Communism fit the current practices in developed countries: concern for safety, clean and well-lighted working places, and efforts to make work interesting for each individual. In countries ruled by the "vanguard of the working classes," however, the workplaces were more often than not dirty, uncomfortable, unpleasant, and unsafe.

Another feature of Communist societies was an abundance of prohibitions and restrictions. "In the West, anything that is not expressly forbidden, is permitted; under Communism, anything that is not explicitly permitted is forbidden," said one popular joke. One had to obtain multiple permissions and approval stamps from state and party agencies for all kinds of activities and undertakings. If you felt sick with a flu or a cold, you could not stay home for a few days: you had to go to your assigned doctor, wait there sometimes for hours, and then get his or her permission not to go to work.

To add insult to injury, Communist mass media continued to extol the virtues of socialism and to condemn the evils of the West. Newspapers contained endlessly tedious speeches by Communist dignitaries and diatribes against "antisocialist forces," "imperialist powers," or "hostile mili-

People living in Communist countries grew used to having decisions made for them by the government. Education, child care (above), and medical care, though free, did not meet Western standards.

tary-industrial circles." In reporting on developments in Western countries, journalists would point only to negative aspects and never mention the positive ones.

Last but not least was the ever-present fear. Except in the most oppressive periods, it was not a fear for your life, but rather a fear of losing your job, of having your children barred from higher education, of being denied permission to travel. It was a state of being afraid to speak up, of always lowering your voice when talking about politics in public places, of feeling your stomach tighten whenever you had anything to do with a policeman, of avoiding any political conversation on the telephone, and never writing anything "dangerous" in letters. Actually, only some phones were bugged and some letters opened, but you never knew whether yours would be among them.

How did people cope with all these indignities? One important haven was culture, which often provided the only refuge and sense of normality. Most Eastern Europeans are avid book readers, and people would often stand in long lines to buy a book by a popular Western author. Public readings of poetry were the Russian specialty. Theaters were generally less subject to censorship, and, in various periods, political cabarets flourished. Political satire was muted, but it was often enough to make a simple gesture or to say a few well-chosen words and the audience understood.

People also turned to foreign broadcasts, particularly to Radio Free Europe and Radio Liberty, U.S. government stations that broadcast in all Eastern European languages. In the late 1980s, these transmissions played a crucial role in the unraveling of Communist regimes.

In the central European countries, political humor was an important means by which to keep one's mental balance. Political jokes, often quite

In Communist societies, the governments used fear to keep people in line. Reform-minded demonstrators always risked being arrested by uniformed or undercover police.

mordant and brutal, lightened up the daily grayness and made it easier to bear the constant flow of irritations. In the more oppressive periods, it could be quite dangerous to tell a political joke; even in more lenient times, you had to be careful in front of whom you spoke. The jokes made fun of inept functionaries ("Who is the most sincere politician in the world? Miloš Jakeš [party chief in Czechoslovakia], because he looks like an idiot, speaks like an idiot, and is an idiot."), of dumb policemen, of the Soviet Union, of all official pretensions and lies ("What is socialism? A tortuous way from capitalism to capitalism."). When family and friends met, the newest political jokes were always a welcome part of the conversation—even among party functionaries themselves.

And finally, there was religion. The "scientific" teachings of Marxism-Leninism were supposed to replace the old religious "superstitions" that, according to the official Marxist propaganda, had only served to oppress and exploit the masses. Marx's slogan "religion is the opium of the people" was one of the key dogmas. The Communist leaders of Albania even closed down all places of worship in 1967. Yet religion survived, despite persecutions. Poland continued to be a devoutly Catholic country, the Protestant church in East Germany headed an unofficial peace movement in the 1980s, Soviet Jews were in the forefront of the dissident movement, and there was an underground church in Czechoslovakia.

Communism, Nazism, and the Democratic West

The birthplace of both Communism and Nazism was Germany. These totalitarian phenomena were both deeply anti-democratic and cruel; both put millions of people to death. They both used modern technology to further their goals: Hitler, for instance, was the first politician to take advantage of flying in order to make several political speeches a day in var-

11

ious parts of Germany. Concentration camps were invented in the Soviet Union and "perfected" by Germans; brainwashing was more thorough under Communism. Stalin and Hitler shared a number of personal characteristics: they both suffered from inferiority complexes, for which they compensated by destroying their real and imagined enemies wholesale; they were fans of American movies and would watch them into early hours; they were both megalomaniacs with a love for huge, ornate buildings and monuments.

The main difference between Communism and Nazism is their starting point: the Marxist idea of an equitable society has been more generally acceptable than the Nazi idea of race as the supreme factor. Nazism is so much connected with white Europeans as a "master race" that you can hardly imagine an Indian or Arab embracing Nazi ideals. Communism, on the other hand, had a much wider appeal and was adopted, in various forms, by nations all across the world, from China to Latin America.

Although Marxism eventually became identified with Soviet Communism, early on, especially in the beginning of the 20th century, it exerted a profound impact on most of Europe and even on the United States. The development of strong labor unions can be traced to Marx's ideas, as can the rise of European social democratic parties.

For decades, the ideas of socialism and Communism attracted Western intellectuals—in fact, before World War II, it was considered fashionable to be leftist and reactionary to be anti-Communist. Many writers and artists hailed the Soviet Union as the country of the future. An American journalist, John Reed, witnessed the October Revolution in Russia in 1917 and wrote his *Ten Days That Shook the World*, which became one of the bibles of the Communist world. He was virtually unknown in the United States until his life story became publicized in the popular film *Reds* (1981).

After World War II, Communism turned into a dirty word in the United States. The prestige of the Soviet Union, the "first socialist country," suffered one blow after another: the revelation of Stalin's crimes in Khrushchev's secret speech in early 1956; the suppression of the Hungarian uprising in late 1956, the occupation of Czechoslovakia in 1968; the publication of *Gulag Archipelago* by Solzhenitsyn in 1974; the invasion of Afghanistan in 1979. By the time Gorbachev came to power in 1985, Communism had very few admirers indeed.

The Fall of Communism

In the spring of 1989, only a very few people sensed the approaching drama. The Communist world was changing, but it looked as if the changes would be gradual and slow. Soviet *perestroika* was in its fourth year. In Poland, Solidarity was being readmitted onto the political scene. The disintegration of Communism in Hungary was proceeding without any great upheaval. The rest of Communist Europe—East Germany, Czechoslovakia, Romania, Bulgaria, and Albania—seemed firmly in the grip of hard-liners. Yugoslavia occasionally appeared in the news as the country with ethnic problems, but only those familiar with that region envisioned the possibility of an approaching bloodbath.

When Hungarian officials cut the barbed wire at the Hungarian-Austrian border in early May, it made only minor headlines. In late sum-

The transformation from a command economy to one controlled by market forces has created great job insecurity among many workers—workers who then agitate for a return to the "old days."

mer, however, after Poland installed its first non-Communist prime minister and the exodus of East Germans to the West picked up speed, the world began to tune in. Television was a crucial protagonist in the happenings, speeding up the upheaval that would change the face of Europe and the world.

The sequence of key events is well-known: demonstrations in East German cities in the early fall; the opening of the Berlin Wall on November 9; the demise of the Bulgarian Communist leadership; the "velvet revolution" in Czechoslovakia; and the bloody clashes in Romania, which culminated in the trial and execution of the Ceauşescus. The two remaining Communist regimes in Europe, Albania and Yugoslavia, began to unravel in January 1990.

Meanwhile, economic hardship and disintegration of political authority continued to undermine the position of Mikhail Gorbachev in the Soviet Union. The year 1991 began with a violent crackdown in the Baltic Republics to suppress calls for independence. In April, Gorbachev and leaders of nine Soviet republics agreed to prepare a new union treaty, giving individual republics much greater autonomy. In June, Boris Yeltsin became the first-ever popularly elected leader of Russia. And then, on August 19, the whole world held its breath when the news about Gorbachev's ouster broke out. Within 24 hours, however, the initial fear dissipated as the plotters turned out to be a rather pathetic group of bunglers. The most exhilarating picture of those days was the indomitable Boris Yeltsin on the steps of the Moscow "White House"; the saddest moment was the speech by a shaky Gorbachev, in which he promised to fight for the renewal of the Communist Party. The bold visionary who had attempted to free the Soviet Union from its past was suddenly overtaken

A botched coup by Soviet hard-liners in August 1991 hastened the collapse of the Soviet Union. A shaken Mikhail Gorbachev (above, returning to Moscow after the coup) resigned on December 25, 1991, and the Soviet Union passed into history.

by history. The final dismemberment of the Communist superpower was orderly; the Soviet Union ceased to exist on December 21, 1991.

Who was the main catalyst of the collapse? President Ronald Reagan, who through the U.S. military build-up put a tremendous pressure on the Soviet Union? Or was it Mikhail Gorbachev, with his courage and vision? Both played a key role, but even more important was the general political disillusionment, cynicism, feelings of hopelessness, corruption, shortages, and inefficient production, and the increasingly defiant population in the European satellites. Ugly shabbiness marked the daily life of the people, from the industrial cities in East Germany to the cotton plantations of Uzbekistan. The glorious dream turned out to be a failure.

Communists After Communism

For all intents and purposes, Communism as a system has disappeared, even though Communist regimes still exist in China, Vietnam, North Korea, and Cuba. These regimes are undergoing multiple changes too, and in many ways are becoming quite capitalist.

In most former Communist countries, Communists and reformed Communists are in high political as well as economic positions. Many of them have proved to be capable managers who now, instead of promoting Marxism-Leninism, talk about privatization, individual enterprise, and stock markets. Not all Communists are the same: for instance, the Hungarian prime minister Gyula Horn, who had initiated the opening of Hungarian-Austrian border in May 1989, resembles a Western European social democrat more than his Communist colleagues in Russia do. Even in Russia, Communists are in a different position than before. They do appeal to older generations, but they are just one of many parties and simply do not have the power to become the sole masters as they were before.

There are two basic ways to look at the post-Communist developments. One is to stress all the negative phenomena; the other is to consider the changes in recent years. And while there are more than enough negative and bad developments, the positive changes are not at all negligible. Optimists would argue that the latter point to the future, not the former.

In many parts of the formerly Communist world, ethnic strife that had long been suppressed reemerged and ultimately blossomed into full-scale civil wars.

Former Yugoslavia and Other Battlefields

Karl Marx, the father of Marxism, was so focused on the economic plight of the working classes that he completely disregarded national or ethnic allegiances. This proved to be one of the major gaps in the Marxist theory. Claiming to be "international" (which meant being subservient to Moscow), the Soviet system suppressed and punished all "nationalist leanings"; it is thus no wonder that a series of ethnic conflicts flared up when the Communist grip weakened. Apart from Moldova and Tajikistan, the heaviest fighting has occurred in former Yugoslavia and the Caucasus.

Former Yugoslavia

The land of South Slavs came into existence in 1919 as the "Kingdom of the Serbs, Croats, and Slovenes," eventually abbreviated to the "Kingdom of Yugoslavia" in 1929. This multiethnic conglomeration was often described as *one country* with *two alphabets* (Latin and Cyrillic), *three religions* (Catholicism, Eastern Orthodoxy, and Islam), *four languages* (Serbo-Croatian, Slovenian, Macedonian, and Albanian), *five nationalities* (Serbs, Croats, Slovenians, Macedonians, and Albanians), and *six constituent republics* (Serbia, Croatia, Slovenia, Bosnia and Herzegovina, Macedonia, and Montenegro).

The tension between the Roman Catholic, Western-oriented, and pro-German Croats on the one hand, and Eastern Orthodox Serbs on the other, goes far back: they have fought each other many times. Serbs also somewhat masochistically commemorate their defeat by the Muslim Turks at the Battle of Kosovo in 1389, when their centuries-long subjugation to the Ottoman Empire began. There are more recent memories, however, that have been resurrected since 1990.

In 1941, Nazi Germany invaded Yugoslavia. Hitler placed Serbia under direct German rule and made Croatia, together with Bosnia and Herzegovina, a puppet pro-Nazi state. Under the government of the Ustasha movement, this state then waged a massive campaign of genocide against Jews and Serbs. A division of Bosnian Muslim collaborators, led by the Nazi SS, became notorious during the war for its ferocity. About 700,000 Serbs died in the Croatian concentration camp of Jasenovac. Meanwhile, Serbian guerrillas known as "Chetniks" began to fight both the Germans and the Croats. By the end of the war, about 1.7 million Yugoslavs had been killed.

Postwar Yugoslavia was ruled by the Communist guerrilla hero, Josip Broz Tito, a Croat born in Bosnia, who used all his authority and power to transform the quarrelsome nationalities of the country into one nation, Yugoslavia. The ethnic harmony born at that time was real, and people were slowly forgetting old animosities; unfortunately, it was fragile: the old hatreds were not buried long enough. When Tito died in 1980, those with a deeper knowledge of Yugoslavia began to fear an explosion.

The first indication of things to come was the 1986 memorandum, published by the Serbian Academy of Sciences, on the existential endangerment of Serbs. The document, charging that the Slovenes, Croats, and Albanians were trying to destroy the Serbian nation, proposed to create "Greater Serbia" to counter this threat. This Serbia was to include all territories inhabited by Serbs—although the complex mosaic of settlement patterns in Yugoslavia made it impossible to carve out "pure" ethnic areas.

The Yugoslav Federation started to come apart in 1990. That summer, the Croatian parliament limited the rights of ethnic Serbs in Croatia, which in turn provoked stringent propaganda from Belgrade, the Serbian capital. The Communist president of Serbia, Slobodan Milošević, had by that time apparently decided that the best way to stay in power was to turn from Communism to nationalism. He embraced the idea of "Greater Serbia" and began to support, ideologically and materially, Serbs outside Serbia proper.

War in Croatia. Even before Croatia declared independence from the Yugoslav federation, on June 25, 1991, violent encounters began in areas with large Serbian population. Out of 4.6 million inhabitants of Croatia, about half a million were Serbs, most of whom lived in the eastern region of Krajina. In July 1991, the war started in earnest. Incited by rhetoric emanating from Belgrade, Croatian Serbs burned and bombed Croatian homes and forced about 200,000 Croats to flee; some 50,000 went to Hungary and the rest to inner Croatia. From there, in turn, Serbs fled to Krajina.

Meanwhile, Europe and the United States tried to stop the killing; after a series of negotiations, a U.N.-sponsored cease-fire took effect on January 2, 1992. A 14,000-member peacekeeping force was sent in to

Sarajevo endured almost constant bombardment during the war in Bosnia. With basic services destroyed, residents of the city were forced to wait in line to collect water and other commodities.

protect the Serbian population and monitor the cease-fire. Serbs, however, remained in control of one-quarter of Croatia, calling it the Republic of Krajina. The six-month war cost about 10,000 lives, created hundreds of thousands of refugees, and caused widespread material destruction.

For the next three and one-half years, Croatia itself was in an uneasy peace. It became involved in fighting in Bosnia and Herzegovina, however, first supporting Bosnian Croats against Muslims and then helping establish the Croat-Muslim Federation in Bosnia. The Croatian president, Franjo Tudjman, was increasingly playing up the Croatian nationalist tune. Tudjman had started his career as a Communist, but in 1967 he was accused of "nationalist opinions" for advocating the use of the Croatian version of Serbo-Croatian language. In 1972, he was sentenced to two years in prison for these attitudes. In 1981, he went to prison for his "Ustasha opinions" and his public claim that only about 70,000 Serbs, and not the 700,000 generally stated, perished in the concentration camp of Jasenovac.

During 1994, Slobodan Milošević began to tire of the war and started urging the Krajina's Serbs to negotiate a settlement with the Croatian government, a plea they ignored. One year later, when the Croatian army attacked Krajina, Milošević turned away from them. Unopposed, Croats reconquered the Serbian-held Krajina within four days and, this time, the refugees were Serbs fleeing to Serbia—at least 150,000, but perhaps 200,000. Croatian soldiers stood by and jeered. Meanwhile, the Croatian media hailed President Tudjman as the "Croatian Bismarck," "Father of the Nation," "Hero of All Heroes," and "Wise Helmsman."

War in Bosnia and Herzegovina. The Bosnian population was a complex ethnic mosaic, with hundreds of thousands of mixed neighborhoods and marriages. Before the war, out of every 10 inhabitants of Bosnia, 5 were Muslims, 3 were Serbs, and 2 were Croats. The Muslims are ethnic Slavs who accepted Islam in the late Middle Ages. Generally, they have been more peaceful than either the Croats or the Serbs.

Following the cease-fire in Croatia in early 1992, the Yugoslav front was quiet for the next three months. In April, however, a war began in Bosnia and Herzegovina, after that republic proclaimed independence. The quick international recognition of the new republic did not help. As early as April, Bosnian Serbs began to massacre Muslims and, by the summer, news about concentration camps and "ethnic cleansing" were making headlines.

In 1993, Bosnian Croats entered the fray as well and fought Muslims in western Bosnia. Early the next year, however, they and the Muslims decided to create a common front against the Serbs.

That war lasted for almost three and one-half years, resulting in 200,000 to 300,000 dead and up to 2.5 million refugees. It was a European nightmare, reported on in detail and full of unbelievable atrocities. One particularly cruel weapon was the systematic raping: Serbian soldiers raped up to 30,000 Bosnian women, to humiliate and frighten them, and to break Muslim resistance. The leader of Bosnian Serbs, Radovan Karadžić, has been indicted by the International Tribunal in The Hague as a war criminal, an indictment he scorns. He no longer has Milošević's support, however, and so is vulnerable and could be arrested if he leaves Bosnia. His colleague and rival, General Ratko Mladić, was responsible for the systematic terror against civilians. He has been also indicted at The Hague.

International Efforts at Peace Settlement. Milošević's Yugoslavia was punished by an embargo, and was even expelled from the United Nations; still, until the summer of 1995 the international community seemed helpless to stop the war. The United Nations sent in a humanitarian peacekeeping force, in July 1992, to get relief supplies to civilians, to protect the so-called "safe areas" (Muslim enclaves within Serbian-held Bosnia), and to help in peace negotiations. They did not have the mandate to fire, which complicated their mission, but they did accomplish an important task: without them, there would have been many more civilian casualties. In June 1995, about 22,500 U.N. troops were operating in the country. They did not include any Americans.

Meanwhile, one peace plan after another failed. In the spring of 1995, the fighting escalated when Bosnian Serbs conquered several "safe areas." In the late summer, the United States stepped in with a two-pronged strategy: vigorous pursuit of settlement, backed by aggressive military action. NATO began its mass bombing of Serbian air-defense systems, and a tough negotiator, Richard Holbrooke, was sent in to broker peace. After much bullying, he managed to bring the presidents of Bosnia

In late 1995, American diplomats finally forced the leaders of the warring Yugoslavian factions to the table. The resulting peace accords are being implemented under the supervision of NATO troops.

and Herzegovina, Serbia, and Croatia to the United States, and then almost physically forced them to reach an agreement.

It is difficult to say whether the war could have been prevented. There are arguments that this or that should have been done and that this or that should not have been done, and the arguing will continue for many years. In the United States there was a strong consensus that Serbs were the main aggressors, while in Europe the attitudes have been more ambivalent, placing the blame on all sides. The most paradoxical perception of all is that Serbs have felt themselves to be the chief victims of the Balkan war.

Joint Endeavor. The Dayton Agreement, signed in Paris on December 14, 1995, consists of the following points:

• Bosnia and Herzegovina will remain one state, with a central constitutional authority, but consisting of two parts, one controlled by

Serbians and the other a Muslim-Croat Federation. How this unusual and unprecedented arrangement will work is anybody's guess.

- Sarajevo will remain one undivided city.
- Refugees will be allowed to return to their homes.
- Indicted war criminals will leave the political arena.

Almost everyone agrees that the peace agreement is not just, but it may be the only feasible one.

A multinational force under the leadership of NATO, called Joint Endeavor, will watch over the implementation of the agreement. The force will consist of 60,000 soldiers from 25 countries, with the largest contingents from the United States (20,000 troops) and Great Britain (15,000). Seven former Communist countries, including Russia, are participating in this mission. The first troops began arriving in early December 1995.

The Former Soviet Union

Considering the vastness of the country, its ethnic complexity, and the fundamental character of changes since the late 1980s, it is almost surprising that there was not more violence in the disintegrating Soviet Union. True, there were bloody clashes—for instance, when Soviet soldiers fired into a crowd of nationalist demonstrators in Georgia in April 1989, or when Uzbeks and Meshketians clashed in June 1989—but these were relatively few and the number of victims was in dozens, not the hundreds or thousands. But even adding the casualties of later fighting in Moldova, Tajikistan, and the Caucasus, the death of the Soviet Union has so far been less painful than its birth. Indeed, from 1917 to 1922, well over 1 million people perished.

Moldova was the only European area of the former Soviet Union that saw prolonged fighting. This conflict had its origin in Stalin's predilection to draw borders in Soviet republics in such a manner as to put together inconsistent parts. While western Moldova had historically belonged to Romania, the eastern part, on the left bank of the River Dnestr, had always been Russian. In the initial euphoria after gaining independence, the Moldovan leaders toyed for some time with the idea of reunification with Romania, a concept that frightened Russians and Ukrainians living in the east. They in turn declared their own independence, and the Moldovan government sent in troops to suppress this move. Fighting erupted in March 1992 and ended in late summer, when a peacekeeping force from the Commonwealth of Independent States came in. Several hundred people were killed. Subsequently, the Trans-Dniester region received an autonomous status and the conflict subsided. One person who played an important role in this settlement was the general of the Russian peace-keeping army, Aleksandr Lebed, who in late 1995 became one of the most talked-about and popular potential candidates for 1996 Russian presidential elections.

Tajikistan. Bloodier than Moldova was Tajikistan, a Central Asian republic inhabited by Indo-European Tajiks, who are close cousins of Afghans. A civil war in that country raged for more than a year, from late 1991 until early 1993, with hard-line Communist forces on one side and Islamic fundamentalists and some democratic groups on the other. This division is somewhat simplistic, however, because more than just politics and religion were involved: it was also a war between the country's historic clans. The conflict cost about 2,000 lives, and some 60,000 Tajiks fled into exile. Because of Tajikistan's remoteness, the world knew much less about this conflict than about Yugoslavia, for instance. It was not a television war.

The fighting ended at the beginning of 1993 and a pro-Moscow regime was installed, supported initially by 8,000 Russian border guards; another regiment protected the capital. By 1995, the number of Russian troops in Tajikistan had risen to 25,000. They are still in the country, patrolling the 665-mile border with Afghanistan in order to stop the spread of Islamic fundamentalism. Islamic fighters, covertly supported by Afghanistan's regime, continue their raids.

The Caucasus has been the most violent region of the former Soviet Union, with three centers of violence: Armenia versus Azerbaijan, ethnic groups in Georgia, and Chechnya.

In late 1994 and early 1995, the breakaway Russian republic of Chechnya became the scene of intense fighting when Russian troops moved into Grozny, the Chechen capital.

The Armenian-Azerbaijani war, mostly over the enclave of Nagorny Karabakh, but in more general terms a struggle between two neighboring hostile nations that harbor centuries-old animosities, began in early 1988. Nagorny Karabakh is a small enclave within Azerbaijan, with a mostly Armenian population. Clashes in the enclave were followed by armed conflicts in other places; by 1992, there was a full-scale war. The following year, Armenia had overrun great parts of Azerbaijan territory outside Nagorny Karabakh, actions that were internationally criticized—even though the world's sympathies were initially mostly with Armenians.

Since a cease-fire in May 1994, negotiated by Russia, a stalemate has persisted. Moscow got a reward for its help in quieting down the conflict: Armenia has allowed Russian military bases on its soil.

In Georgia, several conflicts went on simultaneously. One was between the supporters and opponents of the first popularly elected leader of any Soviet republic, Zviad Gamsakhurdia, a former dissident and fierce Georgian nationalist, who became president in May 1991, with the support of 87 percent of the votes. His anti-Russian policies drove Russians out of Georgia and set the stage for an armed conflict between the dominant Christian Georgians and the two Muslim minorities, Ossetians and Abkhazians. By the fall of 1991, a civil war had erupted, finally forcing Gamsakhurdia to flee the capital. He continued in his resistance until December 1993, when he allegedly committed suicide.

Gamsakhurdia was replaced by the internationally known Eduard Shevardnadze, who has tried since his arrival to Georgia in March 1992 to bring peace to his native land. Ossetia, in the north, calmed later that year, not surprisingly with the help of Russia. Shevardnadze has spent much of his time on the front lines, and once even fled at the last minute, during the siege of Sukhumi, in Abkhazia. A cease-fire in that province was negotiated in May 1994; several months later, Georgia signed an agreement that allowed Russian bases on its soil for 25 years. Georgia badly needs peace; this beautiful country, with stunning architecture in the capital of Tbilisi and a vivacious people known for their love for food and drink, has been ruined almost beyond recognition.

Chechnya was the scene of the most recent flare-up in the region, in early 1995. Chechnya, one of the republics of the Russian Federation, has been pushing for independence for several years. The tension with Moscow brewed for some time and, in early December 1994, Russian troops intervened. It was a badly mishandled operation from the very beginning; it was also the first Russian "television war," bringing bloody scenes into the living rooms of millions of Russians. The decision to intervene was taken by Boris Yeltsin and a small group of insiders, apparently to placate the hard-liners, but the conflict eventually turned against Yeltsin. About 50,000 people perished, and many cities and villages were destroyed. The provisional settlement of the conflict, negotiated by prime minister Chernomyrdin in July 1995, stopped the fighting, but did not bring any lasting solutions. Chechnya continues to be a dangerous spot. Still, the negotiations provided another proof of how the Soviet Union has changed. With minimal democratic experience, Russia is finally learning the art of political compromise.

All post-Communist conflicts have been based on a mixture of historical feuds, religious differences, economic grievances, and ongoing power struggles between groups and individuals. Unfortunately, such conflicts are all too common around the world. In all the struggles discussed here, negotiations have played an important role. This represents an important—and positive—change. When the Soviet Union suppressed the Hungarian uprising in 1956 or invaded Afghanistan in 1979, no negotiation was possible.

European Integration

After World War I, the establishment of a European federation was proposed to the League of Nations by the French minister of foreign affairs, Aristide Briand; his proposal was vague and the idea came ahead of time. Instead of becoming united, Europe soon split up into three large blocks: the Western democracies, Nazi Germany and its allies, and the Communist Soviet Union.

The flag of the European Community includes a star for each member nation—a design somewhat akin to that of the U.S. flag.

Immediately after the end of World War II, during which the West and the Soviet Union had seemingly become friends, there was a brief period of euphoria and a widely shared feeling that harmony and peace would prevail in years to come. European industry, however, was in shambles and a bad drought in 1947 destroyed the harvest. At that moment the United States, whose economy was flourishing, came up with a plan to help all European countries—including the Soviet Union—to rebuild their war-shattered economies.

Named the Marshall Plan, after the U.S. Secretary of State George C. Marshall, this initiative was at the beginnings of modern European integration efforts. In late June 1947, the foreign ministers of the Allied countries arrived to London to discuss the American offer; within a few days, the Soviet representative received orders from Moscow to reject the "imperialist" assistance. Two weeks later, 16 West European nations formed the Committee for European Economic Cooperation, which went on to work out the details of the plan. In early 1948, shortly after the Communists took control of Czechoslovakia in a bloodless coup, the U.S. Congress voted overwhelmingly to get the Marshall Plan going. The assistance was crucial for post-war reconstruction, particularly in Germany.

From that time until the collapse of the European Communist regimes in 1989 and 1990, the term "Europe" was used in the West for just the western half of the continent, with the Iron Curtain forming its eastern boundary. All steps for the creation of greater European unity thus involved only a truncated Europe.

The Committee for European Economic Cooperation, created in 1947 in conjunction with the Marshall Plan, eventually became the Organization for European Cooperation and, still later, in 1961, was renamed the Organization for Economic Cooperation and Development (OECD). This last change reflected the fact that non-European countries—the United States and Canada—had joined the organization.

Meanwhile, the idea of European economic and political cooperation was becoming ever more popular. Its main advocates believed that integration would end the continent's ancient rivalries—between France and England, between Germany and France, and between other countries and regions as well—and replace them with a sense of mutual interest. Furthermore, West European unity was also perceived as a necessary bulwark against the expansionist Communism.

To many people, the 1994 inauguration of the English Channel tunnel connecting Britain and France symbolized the growing unity among the nations of Europe.

The consultative Council of Europe was created in 1949; the first supranational authority in Europe, the Coal and Steel Community, was set up in 1952. It consisted of six countries, Belgium, France, West Germany, Italy, Luxembourg, and the Netherlands. In the spring of 1957, this group signed a treaty in Rome creating the European Economic Community. Three countries, the United Kingdom, Ireland, and Denmark, joined the original six in 1973; Greece became a full member in 1981, and Spain and Portugal joined in 1986.

This community became generally known as the Common Market; in the late 1980s, it began to prepare ground for a fully free flow of goods, labor, and capital between member nations. In December 1991, a milestone meeting took place in the city of Maastricht, in the Netherlands. That city's name rapidly turned into a synonym for European integration, and the "spirit of Maastricht" was the theme of the day. According to the treaty signed that December, the European Community would be renamed the European Union, and a truly open, unique market involving all 12 countries would come into effect on January 1, 1993. The treaty also contained plans for further integration in social and foreign policy, and for the creation of single European currency by 1999.

Meanwhile, the European landscape was changing. The eastern part of the old continent was discarding its Communist shackles in a major political and social earthquake. The divided Germany reunited in late 1990. Other parts of the Communist world went in opposite directions, splitting into new countries. By 1992, instead of one Soviet Union, there were 16 successor republics; instead of one Yugoslavia, there were four new countries. The disintegration trend was completed by the division of Czechoslovakia into two states on January 1, 1993.

In central Europe, one of the most popular slogans of the first post-Communist period was "return to Europe." These countries—Poland, the Czech Republic, Slovakia, and Hungary—have always felt part of Western civilization and considered their subjugation to the Soviet Union as running against all their history. Thus, from the very beginning of their new post-Communist existence, they began to be interested in joining the European Union, and they soon became associate partners of this organization. Central European countries were eventually followed in associate partnership by the Balkan countries (Romania, Bulgaria, and Albania), the Baltic republics, and even some of the other former Soviet republics.

Ironically, as the interest to become integrated into Western European structures grew in the former Communist block, people in Western Europe became less and less enthusiastic about their unification. In 1993, the European Union agreed to accept four new members, Austria, Norway, Sweden, and Finland, pending national referendums. The following year, only three of them actually joined; the voters in Norway said "no." In mid-1994, for example, some 67 percent of Germans and 68 percent of the British were against a federal Europe. This disillusionment stemmed partly from economic difficulties, continuing unemployment, doubts about the wisdom and even feasibility of a common European currency, but also to a large extent from the feeling of helplessness in the case of the war in Bosnia and Herzegovina. Many people have asked what is the sense of European unity, if Europe can do nothing to stop fighting in its own backyard.

Yet the integration process goes on, pushed forward primarily by Germany and France, the pillars of the European Union. In December 1995, German chancellor Helmut Kohl and French president Jacques Chirac issued a letter in which they reaffirmed their resolution to implement all provisions of the Maastricht Treaty and to enlarge the European Union with countries from the former Communist bloc. An intergovernmental conference is set to start working in 1996 to prepare a detailed scenario for admission of new members. Central European countries meanwhile are practicing their own regional economic cooperation: in 1992, they set up the Central European Free Trade Agreement (CEFTA), with the planned, gradual admission of Slovenia, Bulgaria, Romania, and the Baltic states. Another step in linking the two parts of Europe was taken in December 1995, when the Czech Republic became the first post-Communist country to join the Organization for Economic Cooperation and Development.

In May 1995, during the celebrations marking the 50th anniversary of the end of World War II, the old continent looked like an extended family, with a basic common loyalty but with continuing problems, from minor squabbles about this or that regulation coming from Brussels, the bureaucratic capital of the world, to the war in Bosnia and Herzegovina, fighting in Chechnya, and the uncertainty hovering over the future course of Russia. By the end of the year, the peace settlement in the former Yugoslavia and the massive multinational operation to enforce it, Joint Endeavor, brought fresh hope for the future of the house of Europe. In the coming century, the whole of Europe could well become a prosperous, harmonious continent of many different nations and visions.

	THE SOVIET UNION	ALBANIA	BULGARIA	CZECHOSLOVAKIA	EAST GERMANY
1944-1950	The wartime alliance between the U.S.S.R. and England, France, and the **U.S.** sours and turns into the **Cold War**. The U.S.S.R. helps establish Communist regimes in **Eastern Europe**. In January 1949, the Council for Mutual Economic Assistance (**COMECON**) is set up.	In November 1944, a Communist government under Enver Hoxha is set up. In 1946, Albania becomes a People's Republic. In 1948, Albania severs relations with **Yugoslavia**.	In September 1944, Soviet troops enter the country, and the Communist Party rises to power. In October 1946, a People's Republic of Bulgaria is proclaimed.	In May 1945, Soviet troops enter the country. In free elections in May 1946, the Communists emerge as the strongest party, with 38% of the vote. In February 1948, Communists take power in a bloodless coup. In June 1948, Czechoslovakia is proclaimed a People's Democracy.	In May 1945, **Germany** is divided into four zones; eastern Germany comes under the Soviet rule. Berlin is divided into four sectors. In October 1949, the German Democratic Republic is founded. In 1950, Walter Ulbricht becomes the general secretary of the Communist Party (called German Socialist Unity Party).
1953	**Stalin** dies in March.				A workers' uprising in June is suppressed by the Soviet armed forces.
1955	**Warsaw Pact** is established in May.				
1956	In February, **Khrushchev** denounces **Stalin's** crimes in a secret speech at a party congress and initiates the **de-Stalinization** process.				
1958					
1960	A split between the U.S.S.R. and China becomes public; for the next three decades, the two countries will go through long periods of tension and even open hostilities.				

▲ *Agreements made at the Yalta Conference in 1945 helped shape European history for decades to come.*

In 1956, an anti-Communist ▶ uprising in Hungary was brutally suppressed by Soviet troops.

◀ *During his years as Soviet premier, Nikita Khrushchev tried to reform many aspects of the Communist system. He was ousted from power in 1964.*

HUNGARY	POLAND	ROMANIA	YUGOSLAVIA	THE WEST AND OTHER COUNTRIES	
In October 1944, Soviet troops enter the country. During 1948-49, the Hungarian Workers' Party (Communists) gradually assumes power by breaking up other parties. In August 1949, Hungary is proclaimed a People's Democracy.	In July 1944, Soviet troops enter the country. In January 1947, a bloc of four parties dominated by the Communists wins elections. Subsequently, the Communists (known as the Polish United Workers' Party) assume full power.	In August 1944, Soviet troops enter the country. In March 1945, a Communist-led government is set up. A People's Republic is proclaimed in December 1947.	Led by **Josip Broz Tito**, a war hero, the Yugoslav Communists form a government in March 1945. In 1948, **Tito** refuses to acknowledge **Stalin**'s supremacy, and the Soviet Union breaks relations with Yugoslavia. From then on, Tito pursues an "independent road toward **socialism**."	In March 1946, Sir Winston Churchill coins the expression **Iron Curtain**. In 1947, **U.S.** Congress agrees to help postwar reconstruction of Europe through a program called the **Marshall Plan**. During 1948-49, the **U.S.** and other Allies supply blockaded West Berlin in the Berlin Airlift. In April 1949, **NATO** is established.	1944-1950
			Diplomatic relations between the **U.S.S.R.** and Yugoslavia are restored.	The Korean War, during 1950-1953, claims 54,246 **U.S.** casualties.	1953
					1955
In October, Budapest rises in an anti-Communist revolt, but the uprising is brutally suppressed by the Soviet armed forces. **János Kádár**, with Soviet help, becomes the new leader of the country.	In June, workers riot in Poznań, and Władysław Gomułka becomes the first secretary of the Communist Party; subsequently he introduces some liberal reforms and improves relations with the church.		Yugoslavia denounces the suppression of the Hungarian uprising.		1956
In June, Imre Nagy, prime minister during the 1956 uprising, is hanged for treason.				The **European Economic Community** (Common Market) becomes effective on Jan. 1.	1958
				After one year in power, Fidel Castro has transformed Cuba into a strident Communist state.	1960

Fidel Castro's revolution transformed ▶
Cuba into the first Communist
country in the Western Hemisphere.

1961

The U.S.S.R. installs nuclear missiles in Cuba, but under **U.S.** pressure the missiles are dismantled in October, in the Cuban Missile Crisis.

Albania breaks off relations with the **Soviet Union**, accusing **Khrushchev** of abandoning the true precepts of **Marxism-Leninism**.

In August, the East German army erects the **Berlin Wall** and seals off West Berlin.

1963

In 1961, East Germany built the Berlin Wall ▶ around West Berlin. The wall stood for 28 years as a dramatic symbol of the Cold War.

1964

In October, **Khrushchev** is ousted and replaced by **Brezhnev**.

1965

The New Economic Model, giving individual enterprises more autonomy, is adopted.

1967

Following the Six-Day War, the U.S.S.R. condemns Israel and breaks off diplomatic relations.

The government closes all places of worship and declares the country an atheist state.

At a writers' congress in June, an open criticism of party leadership is voiced.

1968

In August, the U.S.S.R. leads a **Warsaw Pact** invasion of **Czechoslovakia** to crush the **Prague Spring**.

In September, the so-called Brezhnev Doctrine is formulated, justifying the right of the U.S.S.R. to intervene militarily in any Soviet-bloc country "in defense of **socialism**."

Albania formally withdraws from the **COMECON** and the **Warsaw Pact**.

In January, **Alexander Dubček** becomes the first secretary of the party and announces his goal of "**socialism** with a human face." The ensuing period of reform becomes known as the **Prague Spring**; it is crushed in August, when about 500,000 **Warsaw Pact** troops invade the country.

1969

In April, **Dubček** is replaced by Gustáv Husák.

1970

The period of so-called "normalization" begins, during which the party leadership suppresses all opposition to its rule.

Will Stoph, the chairman of the State Council, visits West Germany. It is the first official visit of a high East German functionary to West Germany.

▲
The 1968 "Prague Spring" liberalization movement in Czechoslovakia flourished briefly before being crushed by Warsaw Pact troops.

HUNGARY	POLAND	ROMANIA	YUGOSLAVIA	THE WEST AND OTHER COUNTRIES	
Kádár puts forward the slogan, "Whoever is not against us is with us," in a first effort to heal the division of the country following the 1956 uprising.			The nonaligned movement of Third-World countries is formally inaugurated in Belgrade.	**U.S.** military involvement in Vietnam starts. In April, **U.S.**-trained Cuban exiles attempt to overthrow Castro's regime in the Bay of Pigs invasion.	1961
				In November, President John F. Kennedy is assassinated.	1963
In April, **Khrushchev** labels the Hungarian system "goulash **Communism**."			◄ *In 1963, President Kennedy signed a treaty that banned all but underground nuclear-weapon tests.*		1964
		In June, **Nicolae Ceaușescu** becomes the first secretary of the Communist Party.	Yugoslavia introduces far-reaching economic reforms, providing for workers' self-management.		1965
		Romania is the only Soviet-bloc country that does not break relations with Israel.		Israel is the winner in the Six-Day War with Arab states.	1967
The New Economic Mechanism is introduced in January, providing for economic decentralization.	In the spring, students in major cities riot, protesting censorship and political repression. The government subsequently embarks on an anti-Semitic campaign, and many Jews are forced to leave the country.	Romania supports the **Prague Spring** and denounces the August invasion of **Czechoslovakia** by **Warsaw Pact** forces.	Yugoslavia supports the **Prague Spring** and denounces the invasion of **Czechoslovakia** by **Warsaw Pact** forces.	In the spring, students riot in Paris against the Gaullist regime. In April, Martin Luther King, Jr., is assassinated; in June, Senator Robert Kennedy is shot and fatally wounded.	1968
				In July, the first **U.S.** astronauts land on the moon.	1969
	In December, a shipyard workers' protest is brutally suppressed, and at least 44 people are killed. Gomułka is replaced by Edward Gierek.			West German Chancellor **Willy Brandt** initiates his "Eastern policy" of improved relations with the Communist countries by visiting **East Germany**.	1970

29

1972

The U.S.S.R. and the **U.S.** conclude the SALT I treaty, limiting the number of offensive nuclear missiles.

East and West Germany conclude a treaty on economic, political, and cultural cooperation. The treaty also affirms the inviolability of their borders.

1973

Aleksandr Solzhenitsyn publishes his *Gulag Archipelago,* denouncing the Soviet penal system. Early the next year, he is expelled from the U.S.S.R.

▲
In 1972, U.S. President Nixon and Soviet leader Brezhnev signed the SALT I agreements, which limited the antiballistic missile systems of both countries.

1975

1977

Albania breaks off relations with China, accusing it of "social imperialist" policies.

In January, a human-rights manifesto called **Charter 77** is made public, and the authorities respond with a crackdown.

1978

A short-lived cultural "thaw" is initiated by **Zhivkov's** daughter, Lyudmila Zhivkova.

1979

In late December, Soviet troops invade Afghanistan and install a pro-Soviet government.

The New Economic Mechanism, providing for decentralization of the economic policy-making in agriculture, is introduced.

1980

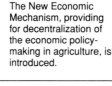
◀ *The U.S. Senate refused to ratify the SALT II agreements, signed by Soviet leader Brezhnev and U.S. President Carter in 1979, when the U.S.S.R. invaded Afghanistan.*

1981

Lyudmila Zhivkova dies, and a period of limited cultural libralization comes to an end.

West German Chancellor Helmut Schmidt visits East Germany.

Nicolae Ceauşescu ruled Romania for 25 years, beginning in 1964. His wife, Elena, was considered the second most powerful person in the country.

President Tito (below right, with an official visitor from China) made Yugoslavia into a relatively liberal socialist country. ▼

1972

In February, **U.S.** President Nixon visits China.

In May, President Nixon visits Moscow; it is the first visit to the **U.S.S.R.** by a **U.S.** president.

1973

In January, Britain, Ireland, and Denmark join the **European Economic Community**.

In September, the Marxist government of Chile is overthrown.

1975

In August, 35 countries sign the **Helsinki Accords**, pledging inviolability of borders and respect for human rights.

1977

About 35,000 miners in the Jiu Valley strike because of economic grievances.

1978

Hungary establishes diplomatic relations with the Vatican.

In October, the archbishop of Cracow, Karol Cardinal Wojtyła, becomes Pope **John Paul II**.

1979

In June, **John Paul II** visits Poland.

The government introduces the New Economic-Financial Mechanism, providing for workers' self-management.

In 1981, Poland's Solidarity movement became the first independent trade union to be recognized in the Communist bloc. ▼

In January, the **U.S.** and China establish diplomatic relations.

1980

Workers begin to strike, and, in August, form an independent labor union, **Solidarity**. The strikers are led by **Lech Wałęsa**.

In November, **Ronald Reagan** is elected president of the **United States**.

1981

In February, General **Wojciech Jaruzelski** becomes prime minister.

Dec. 13, **Jaruzelski** declares martial law, arrests the leadership of **Solidarity**, and suspends the union.

In January, Greece becomes a full member of the **European Economic Community**.

In March, Pope **John Paul II** barely escapes an assassination attempt.

THE SOVIET UNION	ALBANIA	BULGARIA	CZECHOSLOVAKIA	EAST GERMANY

1982

Brezhnev dies in October and is succeeded by Yuri Andropov.

The New Economic Mechanism, providing for decentralization of the economic policy-making in industry, trade, and transport, is introduced.

1983

Italian investigators charge that Bulgarian agents were involved in the attempted assassination of Pope **John Paul II** in March 1981.

The Soviet invasion of Afghanistan turned into a 10-year guerrilla war against well-armed rebels.

1984

Andropov dies in February and is replaced by Konstantin Chernenko.

Between December 1984 and March 1985, the government forces up to 1 million ethnic Turks (Muslims) to adopt Bulgarian and Christian names.

During 1984, 34,982 East German citizens are permitted to emigrate legally to West Germany.

1985

Chernenko dies on March 10 and, the same day, **Mikhail Gorbachev** becomes the new party secretary. He immediately begins his anticorruption and antialcoholism campaign.

In April, Enver Hoxha dies and is succeeded by Ramiz Alia.

The U.S.S.R. was widely ▶ criticized for its secrecy following the nuclear accident at Chernobyl.

1986

In April, a nuclear accident occurs at Chernobyl.

Gorbachev sets up two goals: **perestroika** (economic restructuring) and **glasnost** (political and social opening).

In March, the Italian court rules that there is insufficient evidence to prove Bulgarian complicity in the attempted assassination of Pope **John Paul II**.

In May, East and West Germany sign their first cultural and educational agreement.

Jan.-June 1987

On Jan. 28, the Communist Party Central Committee endorses **Gorbachev**'s proposals for economic and social reforms.

During the year, Albania establishes diplomatic relations with Jordan, Canada, Uruguay, Bolivia, and West Germany (in October).

On April 23, **Honecker** indicates that East Germany would not follow the Soviet model of **glasnost** and **perestroika**.

32

In October, **Solidarity** is effectively dissolved.

In November, **Lech Wałęsa** is released after 11 months of internment.

On July 22, martial law is lifted.

In October, **Lech Wałęsa** is awarded the Nobel Peace Prize.

In July, the government announces a sweeping amnesty.

In October, a popular priest, Jerzy Popiełuszko, is murdered by two secret agents.

▲
In 1983, a May Day demonstration by Solidarity supporters in Gdańsk, Poland, was violently dispersed by police.

In February, four security officers are convicted and sentenced to long prison terms for the murder of Father Popiełuszko.

In November, **Gorbachev** meets with President **Reagan** in Geneva.

In September, the government announces a sweeping amnesty, which affects 71,500 people, including 1,070 political offenders.

▲
Father Popiełuszko, a popular priest murdered by Polish security police, quickly became a hero of the anti-Communist movement.

In January, Spain and Portugal join the **European Economic Community**.

In December, Presidents **Gorbachev** and **Reagan** meet in Reykjavik, Iceland.

John Paul II visits Poland during June 8-14, and openly advocates political pluralism and human rights.

On May 25-27, **Gorbachev** visits Romania, but his speech on **glasnost** and **perestroika** is received without enthusiasm.

In early 1987, Yugoslav media report that there are about 500 political prisoners in the country, mostly ethnic Albanians.

In June, during his visit to West Berlin, President **Reagan** calls on **Gorbachev** to tear down the **Berlin Wall**.

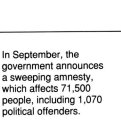

◀ *The Catholic Church, led by John Paul II, the first Polish pope ever, helped inspire the Polish people to challenge Communist rule.*

1982

1983

1984

1985

1986

Jan.-June 1987

33

THE SOVIET UNION	ALBANIA	BULGARIA	CZECHOSLOVAKIA	EAST GERMANY

July-Dec. 1987

On Nov. 2, **Gorbachev** says that **Stalin** had committed enormous crimes.

On Nov. 11, the outspoken **Boris Yeltsin** is dismissed from the Moscow municipal party committee, after being accused by **Gorbachev** of excessive personal ambition and vanity.

In August, an article in the Writers' Union paper *Drita* accuses the Soviet Union of heading toward "barefaced capitalism."

Augustin Navrátil writes a 31-point petition calling for religious freedom. By September 1988, the petition gathers over 500,000 signatures.

On December 17, Gustáv Husák is replaced by Miloš Jakeš as party secretary, but retains his largely ceremonial post of president. In his speech, Jakeš verbally endorses **perestroika**.

During September 7-11, **Erich Honecker** visits West Germany; it is the first visit ever to West Germany by an East German head of state. Honecker pays a visit to his own birthplace in Neunkirchen, and also meets with his sister.

Jan.-Feb. 1988

On Feb. 8, **Gorbachev** announces that the pullout of Soviet troops from Afghanistan will begin on May 15, 1988, and will be completed within 10 months.

On Feb. 11, thousands of protesters in the **Nagorny Karabakh** region in **Azerbaijan** demand reunification with **Armenia**. On Feb. 28, at least 23 Armenians are killed in Sumgait.

Albania raises its diplomatic relations with **Bulgaria** to ambassadorial level.

On Feb. 23-26, Albania participates in the conference of foreign ministers of six Balkan countries in Belgrade. It is an important step out of Albania's diplomatic isolation.

On Jan. 28-29, the Bulgarian Communist Party holds a special party conference to discuss **perestroika**.

On Feb. 29, elections for municipal and regional councils take place; it is the first time that the ballot includes more than one candidate. Over a quarter of the elected deputies are independent candidates, not affiliated with the Communist Party.

On Jan. 11, Miloš Jakeš visits Moscow for talks with **Gorbachev**. The latter says after the meeting that "innovative policies" are needed in Europe.

On Jan. 26-28, West German Chancellor **Helmut Kohl** visits Czechoslovakia; in addition to meeting with the officials, Kohl also meets with representatives of **Charter 77**.

On Jan. 7, **Erich Honecker** begins a three-day visit to France. President Mitterrand and Premier Chirac criticize East German human-rights practices and the existence of the **Berlin Wall**.

On Jan. 17, about 120 persons are arrested during a **dissident** demonstration in East Berlin.

March-April 1988

On March 13, *Sovietskaya Rossiya* newspaper publishes a letter by Mrs. Nina Andreyevna, attacking **glasnost** and **perestroika**. This manifesto expresses the views of hard-line conservative Communists.

In March, several articles tentatively praise certain aspects of the Soviet **glasnost**. At the same time, however, the media criticize as "absurd" the current Soviet condemnations of **Stalin**.

On March 5-6, about 80 persons are arrested during human-rights manifestations in East Berlin and other cities.

May 1988

On May 7-9, a political opposition group known as the Democratic Union is founded in Moscow.

In 1988, many Soviet ▶ people turned out for celebrations marking the one-thousandth anniversary of the introduction of Christianity into Russia.

HUNGARY	POLAND	ROMANIA	YUGOSLAVIA	THE WEST AND OTHER COUNTRIES	
	On Nov. 29, in two related referenda, Polish voters do not endorse political and economic reforms proposed by the government. These are the first referenda ever to take place in a Communist country.	In November and December, antigovernment demonstrations take place in Braşov and several other places. The demonstrators protest against food shortages and restrictions on gas and electricity. On December 14, **Ceauşescu** says at the extraordinary party conference that Romania does not need any changes because it is on a path toward the "radiant summits of **communism**."	Tensions in the province of **Kosovo**, whose population is predominantly Albanian, increase, and, in October, emergency security measures are adopted.	A summit meeting between Presidents **Reagan** and **Gorbachev** takes place in Washington on December 7-10. The two leaders sign the Intermediate-Range Nuclear Forces Treaty and hail the meeting as a success.	July-Dec. 1987
	On Feb. 1, prices of goods and services rise an average of 27%, including 40% increases for basic food, 100% for gas and electricity, and 200% for coal. Protest demonstrations take place in Warsaw and Gdańsk.		On Feb. 24-26, Belgrade hosts a meeting of foreign ministers from **Albania**, **Bulgaria**, Greece, **Romania**, Turkey, and Yugoslavia. It is the first such regional meeting since the early 1930s.		Jan.-Feb. 1988
	On April 25, price increases spark a two-week wave of strikes, the gravest labor unrest since the imposition of martial law in December 1981.	On Apr. 5, the government announces that it intends to reduce the number of Romanian villages from about 13,000 to some 6,000 to 7,000, and replace them with "agro-industrial centers," in the so-called "systematization plan."	On March 14-18, **Gorbachev** visits Yugoslavia and admits that the rift between the **U.S.S.R.** and Yugoslavia dating from 1948 was the Soviet Union's fault.		March-April 1988
On May 14, the first independent trade union (Trade Union of Scientific Workers) is formed. On May 22, **János Kádár** is replaced by Károly Grósz.				Between May 29 and June 2, President **Ronald Reagan** of the **U.S.** visits the **U.S.S.R.** It is Mr. **Reagan's** first visit to the country that he had labeled "an evil empire."	May 1988

35

June 1988

During June 5-16, celebrations of the 1,000th anniversary of the conversion to Christianity are held in the U.S.S.R.

On June 20, **Estonia** officially recognizes the People's Front of Estonia, which becomes the first non-Communist political group to gain official recognition in the U.S.S.R.

◄ *By means of a U.N.-mediated agreement, the U.S.S.R. began to withdraw its troops from Afghanistan in 1988. All the troops were home by mid-February 1989.*

Aug.-Sept. 1988

On Aug. 21, the 20th anniversary of the 1968 invasion, about 10,000 people demonstrate in the center of Prague. It is the largest public protest since 1969, but it is broken up by riot police and tear gas.

Oct. 1988

On Oct. 9, the Latvian Popular Front holds its founding congress.

On Oct. 10, Premier Lubomír Štrougal, the main advocate of economic reforms, is forced to resign.

On Oct. 10, about 80 persons are arrested in East Berlin during a demonstration against censorship of church publications.

Nov. 1988

On Nov. 22, eight people are killed and 126 wounded in violence between **Armenians** and **Azerbaijanis**.

Diplomatic relations with **Hungary** are raised to ambassadorial level.

On Nov. 3, 80 leading intellectuals found the Club for Support of **Glasnost** and **Perestroika.**

Dec. 1988

On Dec. 7, an earthquake registering 6.9 on the Richter scale strikes **Armenia**, killing at least 25,000 people.

◄ *In 1988, a strong earthquake in Armenia caused widespread destruction of property and untold suffering to the people.*

On Dec. 23, Bulgaria stops jamming Radio Free Europe.

On Dec. 1, **Honecker** criticizes the Soviet media for "attempting to rewrite Soviet history in a bourgeois manner."

Between 30,000 and 50,000 Hungarians demonstrate against the Romanian plan to raze as many as 7,000 ethnic Hungarian villages in **Romania** and replace them with agro-industrial complexes.

Local elections take place on June 19, but only 55% of voters participate, which is the lowest turnout since the beginning of Communist rule. **Solidarity** has called for the boycott of the elections.

June 1988

On Aug. 28, Hungarian Premier Grósz meets with the Romanian President **Ceauşescu** in an attempt to resolve disputes between Hungary and **Romania** concerning the Romanian plan to raze ethnic-Hungarian villages. The meeting is unsuccessful.

On Aug. 15, strikes begin in Silesian coal mines and quickly spread to other cities. The strikers demand the legalization of **Solidarity**. On Aug. 31, **Lech Wałęsa** begins discussions with the interior minister, Czesław Kiszczak, and then issues a call to the strikers to return to work.

On Sept. 19, former King Michael of Romania, exiled since 1947, issues a call in Switzerland for a revolt against **Ceauşescu**.

▲
In October 1988, the Polish government announced plans to close the Lenin Shipyard in Gdańsk (above), the birthplace of Solidarity.

Aug.-Sept. 1988

On Oct. 31, the government announces that it will shut down Gdańsk's Lenin Shipyard, birthplace and stronghold of **Solidarity**.

On Oct. 4-6, **Ceauşescu** visits the **U.S.S.R.** During the visit, **Gorbachev** indirectly criticizes Romanian policy and stresses the need for reform.

Oct. 1988

On Nov. 23, Miklós Németh replaces Communist Party Secretary Grósz as premier. Grósz remains general secretary.

Margaret Thatcher visits Poland on Nov. 2-4 and urges the government to start a dialogue with **Solidarity**.

Nov. 1988

Dec. 1988

Jan. 1989

On Jan. 5, the Central Committee of the Communist Party calls for the mass rehabilitation of "thousands of victims" of the Stalinist purges from the 1930s to the early 1950s.

On Jan. 12, **Nagorny Karabakh** is placed under the direct rule of Moscow.

From Jan. 15-20, demonstrations take place in Prague. The police break them up with truncheons, water cannon, tear gas, and dogs. Among those arrested is the **dissident** playwright **Václav Havel**.

On Jan. 15, about 80 people are detained during a silent protest march in Leipzig.

Feb. 1989

By Feb. 15, all Soviet troops have left Afghanistan. In the nine-year war, about 15,000 Soviet troops were killed, and over 1 million Afghan combatants and civilians perished.

On Feb. 21, **Václav Havel** is sentenced to nine months in prison for "inciting anti-state and anti-social activities." Several other **dissidents** are tried on similar charges.

March 1989

In the March 26 elections for the Congress of People's Deputies, many Communist Party candidates are defeated by representatives of unofficial groups of independents. **Boris Yeltsin** wins a landslide victory in Moscow.

April 1989

On Apr. 9, a pro-independence demonstration in Tbilisi, **Georgia**, is brutally attacked by troops; 20 people die, either clubbed to death or killed by toxic gas.

On Apr. 20, **Andrei Sakharov** is elected to the Congress of People's Deputies.

◄ *Mikhail Gorbachev's policies of glasnost (openness) and perestroika (restructuring) have sent shock waves through Soviet society. One side effect of his programs has been the virtual elimination of the personality cult surrounding Lenin, whose statue or portrait once seemed to loom everywhere.*

HUNGARY	POLAND	ROMANIA	YUGOSLAVIA	THE WEST AND OTHER COUNTRIES	
On Jan. 11, a new law establishes the right to form new political parties. The official reevaluation of the 1956 uprising starts with the unauthorized statement by a leading reformer, Imre Pószgay, on Jan. 28, that the 1956 revolt was a "popular uprising," not a counterrevolution.	On Jan. 18, the plenum of the Central Committee of the Communist Party approves a resolution authorizing negotiations with **Solidarity** and its participation in round-table discussions about Poland's future.		On Jan. 11, an opposition party calling itself the Democratic Alliance is inaugurated in Ljubljana, the capital of **Slovenia**. On Jan. 19, the collective state presidency designates Ante Marković the federal prime minister of Yugoslavia.	In January, **George Bush** is inaugurated **U.S.** president.	Jan. 1989
On Feb. 16, the party historical commission publishes a report on the 1956 uprising, which rejects the designation counterrevolution and sharply condemns the Stalinist regimes imposed on the countries in **Eastern Europe**. On Feb. 22, the government announces that the anniversary of the 1917 October Revolution in **Russia** will no longer be celebrated in Hungary.	On Feb. 6, round-table talks between the authorities and the banned **Solidarity** union open. The first session, televised nationally, begins with addresses by the Interior Minister Czeslaw Kiszczak and by the Solidarity leader, **Lech Wałęsa**. In the second half of February, anti-Communist and right-wing opposition groups protest against the round-table talks.		On Feb. 2, a new opposition party called the Initiative for a Democratic Yugoslavia is formed in Zagreb, **Croatia**. Strikes by ethnic Albanians in **Kosovo** lead to resignation of the provincial party leadership; this provokes a Serbian backlash, which culminates in a 700,000-strong demonstration of Serbs in Belgrade against the "chauvinism and separatism" of Kosovar Albanians.	Western governments strongly protest against the sentences given to Czechoslovak **dissidents**, specifically to **Václav Havel**.	Feb. 1989
March 15 becomes the newly designated public holiday, commemorating the start of the 1848 Hungarian uprising against Austrian rule.		In early March, six former high officials accuse President **Ceaușescu** in an open letter of violating human rights and ruining the country's economy. The letter is published in the West on March 12-13.	On March 16, Ante Marković outlines his government program, which consists of a radical transformation of the Yugoslav economy to a free-market system. In early March, Serbian authorities ban public protests in **Kosovo**.		March 1989
On Apr. 22, the Communist Youth Union votes to dissolve itself. On Apr. 25, the **U.S.S.R.** begins a unilateral withdrawal of troops from **Eastern Europe**, starting with Hungary.	On Apr. 6, **Solidarity** and the authorities sign agreements on trade-union pluralism, political reforms, and new economic and social policies. On Apr. 17, **Solidarity** is granted legal status.	On Apr. 12, 1989, the government announces that Romanian foreign debt had been paid back in full.		Student demonstrations in support of democracy start in China in mid-April.	April 1989

May 1989

On May 13-14, over 400 representatives of the Estonian and Latvian Popular Fronts and the Lithuanian Sajudis meet in Tallinn (Estonia) in the first Baltic Assembly.

On May 25, the Congress elects **Gorbachev** to the new post of chairman of the Supreme Soviet (that is, state president).

On May 31, **Boris Yeltsin** criticizes **Gorbachev** for the failures of **perestroika**, and also attacks the **nomenclature** (party and state bureaucracy).

On May 20-21, protests against "bulgarization" by ethnic Turks in north-eastern Bulgaria turn violent. According to official accounts, seven people die, but the unofficial figure is 30.

On May 1, about 2,000 young people stage a pro-democracy demon-stration, but are dis-persed by the police.

On May 17, **Václav Havel** is released from prison after serving four months of his eight-month sentence. The authorities say that he is released because of "good behavior," but Western criticism is a more likely reason.

June 1989

In early June, violent ethnic conflict takes place in **Uzbekistan**, leaving 99 dead and over 1,000 wounded.

On June 16-17, ethnic violence takes place in **Kazakhstan**; the toll is four dead and 53 injured.

During June, over 80,000 ethnic Turks leave Bulgaria for Turkey.

On June 29, a petition called *A Few Sentences* is published. Signed by prominent **dissidents**, but also by many other people, the petition sets out seven demands to "fundamentally change the social and political climate."

July 1989

On July 10, strikes begin in the Kuzbass coalfield in western Siberia. Within two weeks the strikes spread to the Donbass region of eastern **Ukraine**.

On July 27-28, about 300 deputies (including **Boris Yeltsin** and **Andrei Sakharov**) form the "Inter-regional Group" within the Congress of People's Deputies, as an unofficial parliamentary opposition.

By the end of July, over 11,500 people sign *A Few Sentences*.

◀ *Andrei Sakharov, a leading Soviet physicist, emerged as an important dissident in the 1960s. In 1975, Sakharov won the Nobel Peace Prize for his human-rights activities. He spent six years in internal exile for his public opposition to Soviet policies before being released by Mikhail Gorbachev in 1986. In 1989, shortly before his death, Sakharov was elected to the U.S.S.R.'s Congress of People's Deputies.*

On May 2, Hungary begins to dismantle the barbed-wire fence on its border with Austria. This measure reportedly angers the authorities in **Czechoslovakia**, **East Germany**, and **Romania**.

On May 8, **János Kádár** is relieved of his post of party president and of his membership in the central committee.

▲
Hungary's dismantling of the fence on its border with Austria sparked a huge exodus of refugees to the West.

During May 15-18, **Gorbachev** visits China and the state and party relations between China and the **U.S.S.R.** are formally normalized, after almost 30 years of tensions and animosity.

On May 17, over 1 million people participate in the largest antigovernment demonstration in Beijing, China.

May 1989

On June 13 and 21, the Communist Party leadership holds televised roundtable talks with representatives of political opposition groups.

On June 16, Imre Nagy, prime minister during the 1956 uprising, is reburied in a state funeral. The ceremony is attended by some 300,000 people.

On June 4 and 18, the **Solidarity**-backed candidates win a majority in the new National Assembly.

On June 6, **Jaruzelski** invites **Solidarity** to join the government in a broad coalition. Solidarity rejects this offer.

On June 3-4, Chinese troops crack down on pro-democracy demonstrations and kill an estimated 2,000 to 5,000 people in Tiananmen Square.

On June 13, **Gorbachev** and **Kohl** sign a "historic" agreement on human rights and economic cooperation.

June 1989

On July 6, **János Kádár** dies. On the same day, the Hungarian Supreme Court repeals the treason verdicts that were handed down to Imre Nagy and eight of his associates during the 1956 uprising.

On July 11-12, President **Bush** visits Hungary, the first **U.S.** president to do so.

On July 9-10, President **Bush** visits Poland and meets with both **Jaruzelski** and **Wałęsa**. Poles are disappointed with the offered **U.S.** aid because they had expected a larger amount.

On July 19, **Jaruzelski** is elected to the new post of executive president of Poland.

On July 7-8, leaders of the **Warsaw Pact** states meet in Bucharest. Although the final communiqué unanimously endorses the current ideological diversity within the socialist bloc, it is reported that an "unprecedented disunity" reigned behind the scenes.

July 1989

	THE SOVIET UNION	ALBANIA	BULGARIA	CZECHOSLOVAKIA	EAST GERMANY
Aug. 1989	On Aug. 23, more than a million people in **Lithuania**, **Latvia**, and **Estonia** form a 360-mile-long human chain to commemorate the 50th anniversary of the Soviet-Nazi pact of 1939, which set the stage for the Soviet annexation of the **Baltic Republics**.		By Aug. 21, the number of ethnic Turks fleeing from Bulgaria to Turkey has reached 310,000, and Turkey closes its borders.	On Aug. 21, on the anniversary of the 1968 **Warsaw Pact** invasion, several thousand demonstrators clash with the police, and almost 400 people are arrested.	
Sept. 1989	On Sept. 8-10, the People's Movement of the **Ukraine** (referred to as Rukh) holds its founding congress. During September, the **Azerbaijan** Popular Front organizes a blockade of **Armenia**. On Sept. 19, at a meeting of the Central Committee, **Gorbachev** presents a program on nationalities policy, suggesting a restructuring of the Soviet federal system.			About 4,000 East Germans take refuge in the West German embassy in Prague during August and September.	Exodus of East Germans across the newly opened border between **Hungary** and Austria gains momentum; by the end of September, more than 24,000 East Germans have fled. New Forum, an umbrella organization set up to coordinate informal political groups, applies for official recognition, which is denied. Demonstrations start to take place regularly in Leipzig and other East German cities.
Oct. 1989	On Oct. 9, a new labor law recognizes the right to strike; it is the first such recognition in Soviet history. Ethnic tensions continue in **Armenia, Azerbaijan,** and **Ossetia** in Georgia. On Oct. 13, **Gorbachev** strongly attacks certain editors and journalists for abusing **glasnost**. On Oct. 17, the published report by Amnesty International notes that there has been a "dramatic" improvement in the Soviet human rights situation since 1986.	On Oct. 14, the Eco-Glasnost, an environmental group, begins collecting signatures on a pro-conservation petition. On Oct. 18, the Independent Association for the Defense of Human Rights stages its first rally, which is attended by about 160 people. On Oct. 23-24, the authorities start a clampdown on Eco-Glasnost and other unofficial groups, arresting more than 20 people.	On Oct. 28, up to 10,000 demonstrators protest in the center of Prague, and the police detain 355 persons. By the end of the month, the number of signatures on the petition *A Few Sentences* reaches 35,000.		On Oct. 1, a special train with about 4,000 East German refugees leaves Prague for West Germany. On Oct. 4-5, another train with 10,000 to 11,000 East Germans leaves Prague for West Germany. On Oct. 6-7, **Gorbachev** visits East Germany for the celebrations of its 40th anniversary. He reportedly warns **Honecker** that leaders who stay behind "put themselves in danger." On Oct. 18, **Erich Honecker** resigns for "health reasons" and is replaced by Egon Krenz. On Oct. 30, the weekly protest in Leipzig is attended by more than 300,000 people.

On Aug. 24, the parliament elects as prime minister the Catholic intellectual Tadeusz Mazowiecki, a leading **Solidarity** member. It is the end of the Communist era in Poland.

◄ *In August 1989, Tadeusz Mazowiecki (center) was elected prime minister of Poland, the first non-Communist to achieve that position in any Warsaw Pact country.*

Aug. 1989

Roundtable talks between the authorities and opposition groups end in a compromise agreement on Sept. 18. The agreement provides for free elections in 1990.

About 600 East Germans take refuge in the West German embassy in Warsaw during August and September.

On Sept. 12, Mazowiecki forms a new coalition government dominated by **Solidarity** members.

On Sept. 27, the parliament in **Slovenia** proclaims the republic an "independent, sovereign, and autonomous state," with a right to secession from the Yugoslav federation.

During Sept. 9-18, **Boris Yeltsin** visits the **U.S.**, on a private lecture tour.

Sept. 1989

*Huge demonstrations became a ►
regular feature of Czechoslovakia's
"velvet revolution" in late 1989.*

During Oct. 6-10, the Hungarian Socialist Workers' Party (the Communist Party) is fundamentally restructured and renamed the Hungarian Socialist Party. The new party pledges its commitment to multiparty democracy and market economy.

On Oct. 17-20, the parliament approves an amended constitution, describing Hungary as an "independent democratic state."

On Oct. 23, the anniversary of the 1956 uprising, the name of the country is formally changed to the "Republic of Hungary."

On Oct. 10, Poland's first stock exchange opens in Warsaw.

On Oct. 12, the government publishes a plan for a quick establishment of a full-fledged market economy.

On Oct. 26-27, foreign ministers of the **Warsaw Pact** countries meet in Warsaw and announce a new policy of recognizing the absolute right of each state to determine its development.

Oct. 1989

THE SOVIET UNION	ALBANIA	BULGARIA	CZECHOSLOVAKIA	EAST GERMANY

Nov. 1989

On Nov. 4-7, the Armenian National Movement holds its founding congress.

On Nov. 17-19, the Supreme Soviet of **Georgia** reaffirms the republic's right to secede from the Soviet Union.

On Nov. 27, the U.S.S.R. Supreme Soviet grants the **Baltic Republics** full right over their resources and autonomy in financial operations.

On Nov. 28, the Supreme Soviet returns the rule over **Nagorny Karabakh** to **Azerbaijan**.

On Nov. 15, Albania declares an amnesty, which applies to a limited number of political prisoners.

On Nov. 3, about 4,000 people take part in a pro-democracy demonstration outside the National Assembly. It is the largest unofficial demonstration in Bulgaria since 1947.

On Nov. 10, **Todor Zhivkov** is ousted in a "palace coup" and replaced by Petur Mladenov, the foreign minister, who promises to turn Bulgaria into "a modern democratic and law-governed state."

On Nov. 17, an official rally of over 100,000 supports political reforms.

On Nov. 17, an officially approved student demonstration turns into a violent clash with the police.

On Nov. 20, a "demonstration week" begins, with protest rallies growing in numbers and spreading throughout the country.

On Nov. 27, a two-hour general strike is supported by millions of workers.

On Nov. 29, the article guaranteeing the "leading role of the Communist party" is abolished.

On Nov. 4, over 500,000 demonstrate in East Berlin.

On Nov. 7, the whole Politburo of the Communist Party resigns.

On Nov. 8, the New Forum opposition group is legalized.

On Nov. 9, the **Berlin Wall** is opened and several million East Germans visit West Berlin in the first few days.

On Nov. 17, the new prime minister, Hans Modrow, says that speculation about German reunification is "as unrealistic as it is dangerous."

Dec. 1989

On Dec. 1, **Mikhail Gorbachev** meets with **John Paul II**. It is the first meeting ever between a pope and a Soviet head of state.

On Dec. 7, the Lithuanian Supreme Court deletes the article guaranteeing the "leading role" of the Communist Party.

On Dec. 14, **Andrei Sakharov** dies of a heart attack.

On Dec. 19-20, the Communist Party of **Lithuania** declares itself independent of the Communist Party of the Soviet Union.

On Dec. 11, **Zhivkov** is expelled from the Communist Party.

On Dec. 10, a new federal government is formed in which the non-Communists have a majority. The same day, President Husák resigns.

On Dec. 17, the border with Austria is opened.

On Dec. 20, the extraordinary congress of the Communist Party adopts a statement apologizing to the Czechoslovak people for "unjustified reprisals" after 1968.

On Dec. 28, **Alexander Dubček** is elected chairman of the Federal Assembly.

On Dec. 29, **Václav Havel** is elected president of the republic.

On Dec. 1, the parliament abolishes the leading role of the Communist Party.

On Dec. 3, a human chain of up to 2 million people joins hands across East Germany, calling for democratic renewal.

On Dec. 7, roundtable talks are held with the opposition, and the participants agree that general elections will be held in May 1990.

On Dec. 16-17, the Communist Party changes its name from the "Socialist Unity Party" to "Socialist Unity Party—Party of Democratic Socialism."

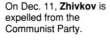

◄ *Millions of East Germans visited West Berlin in the first few days after the Berlin Wall was opened.*

On Nov. 26, a referendum narrowly approves the petition of opposition groups to postpone the election of a president after the legislative elections in March 1990.

On Nov. 20-24, the 14th congress of the Romanian Communist Party is held, and **Ceauşescu** is elected for a further five-year term as the general secretary.

On Nov. 28, West German Chancellor **Helmut Kohl** presents a plan for a German confederation that could eventually lead to reunification.

Nov. 1989

◄ *Romania's overthrow of the Ceauşescu dictatorship was by far the most violent of the 1989 revolutions in Eastern Europe.*

On Dec. 29, the parliament approves a radical economic-reform package, to begin on Jan. 1, 1990.

On Dec. 29-30, the formal name of the country is changed to "Polish Republic" (instead of Polish People's Republic).

On Dec. 16, several hundred people protest a deportation order served on a Protestant pastor, Fr. Lázsló Tökes, in Timişoara. Next day, the protests grow larger, and the police fire on the crowds.

On Dec. 22, **Ceauşescu** and his wife are airlifted from the Central Committee building as demonstrators break in. The rebels form the National Salvation Front (NSF).

On Dec. 25, **Nicolae** and Elena **Ceauşescu** are tried before a military tribunal; condemned to death; and immediately executed.

By Dec. 25, **Ion Iliescu** is named president by the NSF.

On Dec. 28, the country's name is changed to Romania (replacing the Socialist Republic of Romania).

By December, relations between **Slovenia** and **Serbia** deteriorate considerably, leading to the effective closure of the border between the two republics.

On Dec. 2-3, Presidents **Bush** and **Gorbachev** meet aboard **U.S.** and Soviet warships off the coast of Malta for their first summit.

Dec. 1989

▲ *U.S. President Bush and Soviet President Gorbachev developed a friendly rapport during their first summit meeting in Malta.*

THE SOVIET UNION	ALBANIA	BULGARIA	CZECHOSLOVAKIA	EAST GERMANY

Jan. 1990

On Jan. 11, the Supreme Soviet of **Latvia** abolishes the "leading role" of the Communist Party.

On Jan. 11-13, **Mikhail Gorbachev** visits **Lithuania**, on a mission to solve the secessionist crisis.

On Jan. 19, Soviet troops assault the city of Baku, **Azerbaijan**, following the escalation of ethnic violence between Armenians and Azerbaijani that has erupted early in January.

On Jan. 1, Ramiz Alia says in his New Year's message that the country's enemies are renewing "a campaign of slanders" against Albania. He further states that Albania is a "society of "justice" without "social conflicts or national oppression."

According to second-hand testimony, anti-Stalinist demonstrations take place on Jan. 11 and 14 in the city of Shkodër, involving up to 7,000 people.

On Jan. 1-2, anti-Turkish demonstrations break out in southern Bulgaria.

On Jan. 15, the parliament repeals the article guaranteeing the "leading role" of the Communist Party.

On Feb. 2, the 14th extraordinary congress of the Communist Party states in its manifesto that the party is now committed to "human and democratic **socialism**."

On Jan. 2, President **Havel** visits East and West **Germany**.

On Jan. 25-26, President **Havel** visits **Poland** and **Hungary**.

Throughout January, roundtable talks with opposition groups continue.

On Jan. 15, thousands of protesters ransack the headquarters of the secret police in Berlin.

On Jan. 28, Prime Minister Hans Modrow announces the formation of a government of national responsibility, which includes eight opposition ministers.

Feb. 1990

On Feb. 5-7, the Central Committee backs **Gorbachev**'s new platform that clears the way for a multiparty system in the U.S.S.R.

On Feb. 23, the Supreme Soviet of **Estonia** abolishes the article guaranteeing the "leading role" of the Communist Party.

On Feb. 8, after the opposition groups refuse to join a new coalition government, the National Assembly approves a government that consists solely of Communist ministers.

On Feb. 25, the opposition alliance called Union of Democratic Forces organizes a rally at which 200,000 participate.

On Feb. 1, the secret police is abolished.

During Feb. 17-22, President **Havel** visits Iceland, Canada, and the **U.S.**

On Feb. 26-27, **Havel** visits Moscow and confers with **Gorbachev**. They sign an agreement that all 73,500 Soviet troops stationed in Czechoslovakia will depart by July 1991.

On Feb. 1, upon his return from the **U.S.S.R**, Prime Minister Hans Modrow proposes to create a united, neutral **Germany**.

On Feb. 5, the government of national responsibility is installed, with a majority of non-Communists.

On Feb. 13-14, Hans Modrow visits West Germany.

March 1990

On March 11, the Supreme Soviet of **Lithuania** declares the republic independent.

On March 13, the Congress of People's Deputies abolishes the monopoly of the Communist Party.

On March 14, **Mikhail Gorbachev** is elected President of the U.S.S.R.

On March 30, the Supreme Soviet of **Estonia** agrees to set in motion a process of secession from the U.S.S.R.

On March 5, the National Assembly adopts a bill that allows ethnic Turks to resume their original names that they had been compelled to renounce during the forced assimilation in 1984-85.

On March 6, the National Assembly legalizes strikes for the first time in Bulgarian history.

Throughout March, the Federal Assembly is engaged in a "hyphen war"—a prolonged debate about the new name of the country. The Slovaks, inhabitants of **Slovakia** in the eastern part of the country, want the name to be spelled "Czecho-Slovakia," but the Czechs reject this spelling.

On March 18, the first free and secret general elections are held in East Germany. The winning party, the Christian Democratic Union, gets 40.8% of the vote; the Communists get 16.4%.

HUNGARY

On Jan. 5, the "Danube-gate" scandal breaks open when it is revealed that the Interior Ministry security police have not stopped covert surveillance of opposition politicians, despite amendments creating a multiparty system.

By 1990, Lithuanians (above) and other residents of the Baltic Republics had become very vocal in their demand for independence from the Soviet Union.

On March 10, an agreement is signed with the **U.S.S.R.** providing for the complete withdrawal of all 52,000 Soviet troops from Hungary by July 1991.

On March 25, the first round of general elections takes place.

POLAND

On Jan. 27, the Polish Communist Party (named Polish United Workers' Party) decides to disband itself at its 11th and final congress. The gathering then becomes a founding congress of a new party, the Social Democracy of the Polish Republic.

ROMANIA

On Jan. 3, the NSF reverses the former regime's prohibition of foreign borrowing.

On Jan. 12, the NSF outlaws the Communist Party of Romania, but the next day the decision is reversed.

On Jan. 28-29, large demonstrations take place in Bucharest, first by the opponents of the National Salvation Front, and then by supporters.

On Feb. 1, the National Salvation Front agrees to share power with representatives of 29 opposition parties.

On Feb. 18, about 3,000 to 8,000 demonstrators demand **Ion Iliescu**'s resignation. Next day, 5,000 to 8,000 miners from the Jiu Valley are brought to Budapest in support of the National Salvation Front.

On March 1, the Timişoara Declaration calls for the banning of ex-Communists from public offices.

On March 20, about 2,000 Romanian nationalists attack a peaceful demonstration by 5,000 ethnic Hungarians in Transylvania.

YUGOSLAVIA

On Jan. 2, Yugoslavia introduces a new dinar worth 10,000 old dinars, in an effort to bring down inflation, which has reached 1,125% in December.

On Jan. 20-23, the 14th extraordinary congress of the Communist Party (League of Communists of Yugoslavia) takes place, but it ends in disarray after the delegation from **Slovenia** walks out.

At the end of January, violence erupts again in the province of **Kosovo**.

On Feb. 4, the League of Communists of **Slovenia** renounces its links with the League of Communists of Yugoslavia.

THE WEST AND OTHER COUNTRIES

On Feb. 13, the four major World War II Allies—France, the **U.S.S.R.**, England, and the **U.S.**—and the two German states agree on a "two-plus-four" formula for the unification of **Germany**.

On Feb. 25, the opposition candidate wins the presidency in Nicaragua against the candidate of the Sandinistas.

Jan. 1990

Feb. 1990

March 1990

47

April 1990

On Apr. 6-7, an extraordinary congress of the Latvian Communist Party takes place, and ends in a split into independent and pro-Moscow parties.

On Apr. 18, the U.S.S.R. begins an economic blockade of **Lithuania**.

On Apr. 17, Ramiz Alia says at the Central Committee's plenium that Albania is no longer opposed to diplomatic ties with the **U.S.S.R.** and with the **U.S.**

On Apr. 3, Petur Mladenov is elected president of Bulgaria.

On Apr. 3, the Communist Party renames itself the Bulgarian Socialist Party.

On Apr. 9, a meeting of Czechoslovak, Hungarian, and Polish leaders is held in Bratislava, to discuss the "return to Europe" of the three countries.

On Apr. 20, the Federal Assembly adopts the new name of the country: Czech and Slovak Federative Republic.

On Apr. 12, a new "grand coalition" government led by the Christian Democratic Union is sworn in.

May 1990

On May 1, following the May Day parade, about 40,000 people from opposition groups denounce Communist rule and President **Gorbachev**.

On May 4, the Supreme Soviet in **Latvia** proclaims Latvia's independence from the U.S.S.R.

On May 8, the Supreme Soviet in **Estonia** proclaims Estonia independent.

On May 29, **Boris Yeltsin** is elected president of **Russia**.

On May 7-8, the People's Assembly approves judicial and economic reforms and lifts the ban on religious propaganda. According to unofficial reports, there have been demonstrations in several Albanian towns in the previous months.

◀ *At Moscow's 1990 May Day Parade, thousands of demonstrators denounced the Communist government.*

On May 18, a treaty on "the creation of a monetary, economic, and social union" between the two Germanys is signed.

June 1990

On June 12, **Russia** is declared a sovereign state.

On June 20, the Supreme Soviet of **Uzbekistan** declares the republic sovereign.

On June 23, the Supreme Soviet of **Moldavia** adopts a declaration of sovereignty.

On June 29, **Lithuania** suspends its declaration of independence, and Moscow lifts its economic blockade.

On June 10 and 17, free elections are held. The Communist Party, renamed Socialist, receives 47% of the vote.

On June 8-9, the first free elections since 1946 are held. The victors are the Civic Forum in the Czech lands, and its counterpart in **Slovakia**, Public Against Violence, with 47% of the vote. Communists receive almost 14% of the vote.

April 1990

On Apr. 8, the second round of general elections takes place, and the center-right Hungarian Democratic Forum wins 41.6% of the votes.

On Apr. 13, the Soviet authorities admit Soviet responsibility for the Katyn Forest massacre.

On Apr. 19-20, **Solidarity** holds its first major national conference since 1981.

On Apr. 7-8, the NSF meets in its first national conference and calls for a democratic multiparty system.

On Apr. 11, the National Salvation Front bars former King Michael of Romania from entering the country.

On Apr. 8, a center-right coalition called DEMOS wins in the first free elections in **Slovenia**.

On Apr. 22, the first round of elections in **Croatia** takes place.

May 1990

On May 16, Prime Minister Jozsef Antall forms a coalition government.

On May 27, the first fully free elections take place, for local councils. **Solidarity**-backed candidates win 41% of the seats, but only 42% of voters participate in the elections.

On May 20, in the first free elections in Romania since 1937, the National Salvation Front wins 66.3% of the votes, and **Ion Iliescu** wins the presidency with 86% of the votes.

On May 6-7, the second round of general elections takes place in **Croatia**, and the winning party is the right-wing nationalist Croatian Democratic Union.

On May 5, the first round of "two-plus-four" talks on the reunification of **Germany** takes place in Bonn.

On May 29, representatives of 40 countries sign the founding charter of the European Bank for Reconstruction and Development, which is intended to finance the economic rehabilitation of **Eastern Europe**.

June 1990

During June 13-15, violent confrontation takes place in Bucharest between anti-Communist demonstrators and pro-government miners brought into the city. The toll is six people dead and about 500 injured.

Between May 31 and June 3, Presidents **Bush** and **Gorbachev** hold their second summit in Washington.

◀ *In December 1989, dissident playwright Václav Havel was elected president of Czechoslovakia. He received a visit from Pope John Paul II in April 1990.*

49

	THE SOVIET UNION	ALBANIA	BULGARIA	CZECHOSLOVAKIA	EAST GERMANY
July 1990	On July 10, at the 28th party congress, **Gorbachev** is reelected general secretary. On July 11, **Yeltsin** quits the Communist Party.	In early July, about 5,000 Albanians seek refuge in foreign embassies and are eventually allowed to leave the country. On July 31, Albania and the **U.S.S.R.** restore diplomatic relations.	On July 6, Mladenov is forced to quit because of charges that he wanted to use tanks against demonstrations in December 1989.	On July 6, **Václav Havel** is reelected president for a two-year term.	On July 1, East and West Germany become united economically with one currency. On July 16, seven nations (England, France, the **U.S.**, the **U.S.S.R.**, East Germany, West Germany, and **Poland**) agree on unification of the two Germanys.
Aug. 1990			On Aug. 1, **Zhelyu Zhelev**, leader of the Union of the Democratic Forces, is elected president.		
Sept. 1990	On Sept. 13, a new German-Soviet friendship pact is signed, allowing the united **Germany** to play a major role in the changing Soviet economy.				
Oct. 1990	On Oct. 1, the U.S.S.R. Supreme Soviet passes a law guaranteeing full religious freedoms. On Oct. 2, **Lithuania** and the U.S.S.R. agree to conduct their economic relations as equal partners. On Oct. 17, the Ukrainian parliament bows to student demands and agrees to support the Ukrainian independence.			On Oct. 11, thousands rally in Prague in an anti-Communist demonstration. On Oct. 17, Finance Minister **Václav Klaus** is elected chairman of the Civic Forum. He is the most outspoken advocate of a free-market economy.	At the stroke of midnight on Oct. 2, East Germany ceases to exist as it voluntarily merges with West Germany. About 1 million people celebrate at the Brandenburg Gate in Berlin.
Nov. 1990	On Nov. 17, **Gorbachev** presents a new emergency power structure, in which he would rule together with the Federation Council representing the 15 republics. After several days, the plan is rejected by **Yeltsin** as insufficient.		Throughout the month, antigovernment rallies take place in Sofia. The government is forced to resign on Nov. 29.	On Nov. 24, local elections take place; Communists win 17% of the vote.	
Dec. 1990	**Germany** begins air-lifting emergency food supplies to the U.S.S.R. On Dec. 20, **Eduard Shevardnadze** resigns, warning of an "onset of dictatorship."	On Dec. 9, a large student demonstration takes place in Tirana.		On Dec. 12, the Federal Assembly approves a new division of power between the Czech lands and **Slovakia**.	

◄ *In July 1990, thousands of Albanians who had sought refuge in foreign embassies were allowed to leave the country aboard ships sailing under the United Nations flag.*

On July 5, **Serbia** suspends the parliament of **Kosovo**.

◄ *On October 2, 1990, amid much celebration, Germany became a united country for the first time since the end of World War II.*

On Aug. 3, the writer **Arpád Göncz**, member of the Alliance of Free Democrats, is elected Hungarian president.

During Aug. 21-27, antigovernment demonstrations take place in Bucharest.

On Aug. 2, Iraq invades Kuwait.

On Sept. 17, **Wałęsa** declares his presidential candidacy against Mazowiecki.

On Sept. 12, a treaty between WWII Allies and the two Germanys ends the Allied powers' responsibility over **Germany**.

On Oct. 15, the ruling party, Hungarian Democratic Forum, is beaten in local elections. Less than 30% of eligible voters participate.

On Oct. 26, taxi and truck drivers block traffic throughout the country, protesting gas price hikes.

On Oct. 18, the government presents a radical plan for a transition to a market economy.

On December 9, 1990, Lech Wałęsa won the presidency of Poland in a landslide election.
▼

On Nov. 25 Mazowiecki resigns after losing the first round of presidential elections.

On Nov. 19, 35 nations, members of the **Conference on Security and Cooperation in Europe** sign a treaty limiting conventional weapons systems in Europe.

On Dec. 9, **Wałęsa** is elected president of Poland in a landslide victory.

On Dec. 2, **Kohl** is elected chancellor of the united **Germany**.

51

THE SOVIET UNION	ALBANIA	BULGARIA	CZECHOSLOVAKIA	GERMANY
Jan. 1991 On January 7, Soviet military forces begin a crackdown in the **Baltic Republics**; 19 people are killed. On January 20, 100,000 people in Moscow protest the intervention.	The flow of refugees to Greece intensifies in late December and early January. On January 18, the first legal religious service since 1967 takes place in a Tirana mosque.		On January 1, the first package of economic reforms is introduced, including **price liberalization**, "small" **privatization**, and internal convertibility of the Czechoslovak currency.	
Feb. 1991 On February 9, 90% of voters in **Lithuania** endorse independence. On February 22, 400,000 people in Moscow protest against censorship.	Following student strikes and demonstrations, Ramiz Alia declares presidential rule on February 20.	On February 1, the government introduces the first stage of economic reforms by removing price subsidies.	On February 10, Civic Forum, the opposition coalition that brought down the Communist regime, splits into the rightist Civic Democratic Party and centrist Civic Movement.	In former **East Germany**, unemployment rises to 9% by the end of February.
March 1991 In referendums in **Latvia**, **Estonia**, and **Georgia**, most voters support independence. On March 17, in an all-Union referendum, over 75% of voters agree with the preservation of the U.S.S.R. as a "renewed federation of equal, sovereign republics." Six republics do not participate in the referendum.	In the first week of March, about 20,000 shipborne Albanians arrive in southern Italian ports.		On March 6, **Vladimír Mečiar** founds the Movement for Democratic Slovakia, which aims at greater autonomy for **Slovakia**.	German cabinet approves the "joint program for eastern regeneration," earmarking millions of dollars for the next two years to former **East Germany**.
April 1991 On April 23, **Mikhail Gorbachev** and leaders of nine Soviet republics sign a pact paving the way to a new Union treaty and an economic "anti-crisis program."	On March 31 and April 7, in the first free multiparty elections ever held in the country, the Communist Albanian Party of Labor wins a two-thirds majority in the parliament.		On April 23, **Mečiar** is dismissed by the Slovak National Council as head of the Slovak government.	Economic hardships cause a tide of protests in eastern cities. Chancellor **Helmut Kohl** is jeered by several hundred protesters in Erfurt on April 7.
May 1991 In late April and May, conflict between **Armenia** and **Azerbaijan** escalates. On May 26, Zviad Gamsakhurdia is elected president of **Georgia**.			On May 21, the Federal Assembly approves a bill on land **restitution**. ◀ *Private industry has been slow to take hold in formerly hard-line Albania. In Tirana, the country's first private hair salon opened in early 1991.*	On May 20, four former East German high officials are charged for manslaughter in connection with the **Berlin Wall** policy of "**shoot-to-kill.**"
June 1991 On June 12, **Boris Yeltsin** is popularly elected president of **Russia**.			By June 30, the last Soviet troops leave Czechoslovakia.	

52

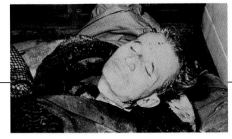

▲
More than a year after the revolution that led to the execution (above) of Nicolae Ceauşescu, Romania was still beset by much turmoil, and its government remained dominated by former Communists.

Jan. 1991

Jan Krzysztof Bielecki becomes new premier of Poland.

Anti-government protests that began in mid-December continue throughout January.

On January 14, the constitutional court of Yugoslavia annuls parts of **Slovenia**'s declaration of sovereignty from July 1990.

On January 25, **Macedonia** declares sovereignty.

Feb. 1991

Railway workers strike throughout February, asking for higher wages.

Energy shortages lead to halting of production in hundreds of enterprises.

On February 20, **Slovenia** initiates "disassociation with Yugoslavia."

On Feb. 24., the Persian Gulf War between the **United States** and its allies and Iraq begins; it ends with Iraq's defeat in April.

March 1991

The Paris Club of 17 creditor countries agrees on March 15 to write off 50% of Poland's debt to foreign governments.

Hundreds of thousands of ▶ mourners turned out to honor the 19 Lithuanians killed when Soviet troops attempted to crack down on the republic's independence movement.

April 1991

Lech Wałęsa travels to Brussels, France, and the United Kingdom to discuss Poland's membership in the **European Community**.

On April 1, the second stage of the **price liberalization** program starts (the first stage began in November 1990).

President Mitterrand of France travels to Romania, the first Western leader to visit since December 1989.

May 1991

On May 16, the Polish parliament (*Sejm*) rejects an anti-abortion bill. By the end of May, unemployment reaches 7.7%.

On May 10, 12 senior officers of the former *Securitate* Secret Police are sentenced to prison terms between 30 months and five years.

Throughout the month, bloody clashes between Serbs and Croats occur in municipalities in **Croatia** that have a predominantly Serbian population.

June 1991

On June 26, the National Assembly approves a bill that offers partial **compensation** to Hungarians for property nationalized after June 1949.

On June 1, Pope **John Paul II** begins his fourth visit to Poland.

On June 17, Poland and **Germany** sign a friendship treaty.

After **Slovenia** and **Croatia** declare independence on June 25, fighting erupts between the Slovenian Territorial Defence and the Yugoslav National Army.

53

July 1991

On July 1, the **Warsaw Pact** is dissolved in Prague.

On July 12, the Grand National Assembly adopts a new constitution that defines Bulgaria as a "democratic, constitutional, and welfare state."

Aug. 1991

On August 19, Soviet hard-liners depose **Mikhail Gorbachev** and send tanks to major cities to overthrow the democratic forces. **Boris Yelstin** heads the opposition to the coup. On August 21, Gorbachev is reinstated. The Supreme Soviet suspends the Communist Party on August 29. By the end of the month, most Soviet republics declare independence.

On August 7-8, about 10,000 destitute Albanians enter the Italian port of Bari. When Italian authorities try to repatriate the **refugees**, fighting erupts.

◄ *Boris Yeltsin heroically led the opposition to the August 19, 1991, coup by Soviet hard-liners.*

Sept. 1991

State Council of the U.S.S.R. recognizes the independence of **Lithuania**, **Latvia**, and **Estonia**.

Anti-Communist demonstrations continue in Tirana.

In Saxony (former **East Germany**), groups of **skinheads** and neo-Nazis attack foreigners, mostly from **Romania**, **Yugoslavia**, Vietnam, and Africa.

Oct. 1991

On October 13, in the second general elections since the fall of the Communist regime, the opposition Union of Democratic Forces closely defeats the Bulgarian Socialist (formerly Communist) Party.

Nov. 1991

The first completely non-Communist government takes office on November 9.

Dec. 1991

On December 21, the U.S.S.R. is replaced by the **Commonwealth of Independent States (CIS)**, a loose alliance of 11 former Soviet Republics. **Mikhail Gorbachev** resigns on December 25.

▲ *Estonia (above) and its fellow Baltic Republics finally gained independence from the Soviet Union in the wake of the botched Moscow coup of August 1991.*

▲ *In the months following German reunification, skinheads and other groups intolerant of foreigners arose in what had been East Germany.*

On December 23, Germany recognizes the independence of **Slovenia** and **Croatia**.

54

▲

A brutal civil war began as the various republics that made up Yugoslavia declared their independence. Violent battles took place in many areas of Croatia (above).

Fighting in **Slovenia** ends on July 3, but violent clashes escalate in eastern **Croatia**.

On July 31, Presidents **George Bush** and **Mikhail Gorbachev** sign the Strategic Arms Reduction Treaty at their third summit meeting in Moscow.

July 1991

Fighting continues in **Croatia**; bombardment of the city of **Vukovar** begins in late August.

Aug. 1991

On September 26, miners striking against inflation get into a violent conflict with security police in Bucharest; the government subsequently resigns.

Croatia cuts off oil supplies to **Serbia** on September 7. Fighting in Croatia continues despite international efforts at mediation.

Sept. 1991

On October 27, free multiparty elections for *Sejm* produce a fragmented legislature; twenty-nine parties are represented, none receiving more than 13% of the vote. Only 43% of eligible voters take part in the elections.

Amid almost constant ▶ bombardment, the people of the Croatian city of Dubrovnik formed long lines to obtain food, water, and other essentials.

Oct. 1991

On November 21, the parliament adopts a new constitution guaranteeing pluralism, human rights, and free markets.

The Croatian town of **Vukovar**, besieged by the Serbian army for three months, falls.

Nov. 1991

On December 7, Hungary becomes the first country to establish full diplomatic relations with **Ukraine**.

On December 5, a new Polish government is formed, headed by Jan Olszewski.

A summit of the **European Community**, on Dec. 9-10, develops the **Maastricht Treaty**, an agreement on a framework for a **European Union**.

Dec. 1991

55

	EUROPEAN UNION (EU)	ALBANIA	BULGARIA ROMANIA	CZECH REPUBLIC SLOVAKIA	HUNGARY
Jan.-Feb. 1992	Unemployment in former **East Germany** reaches 17% in January.	Food riots in January and February result in dozens of deaths.	On January 19, **Zhelyu Zhelev** is reelected president of Bulgaria for a term of five years.	In early February, the Slovak National Council rejects a draft of the federal constitution.	Tensions with **Czechoslovakia** over the Gabčíkovo hydroelectric dam increase in February.

March-April 1992		On March 22 and 29, the Opposition Democratic Party wins in general elections, and, on April 6, **Sali Berisha** becomes Albania's first post-Communist president. *In early 1992, Bulgarians reelected Zhelyu Zhelev (below) to the presidency of Bulgaria. The election features the first large-scale campaigning by candidates in the history of Bulgaria.* ▼	In Romania on March 29, Petre Roman becomes president of the National Salvation Front, which approves his free-market reform program. On April 25-27, former Romanian king Michael visits his country.		

May-June 1992	Greece refuses to recognize **Macedonia** because it claims that the name "Macedonia" is part of Greek heritage.			On May 18, the first round of "large" **privatization** begins. The June 5-6 general elections result in political polarization between the Czech and Slovak republics.	▲ *In March 1992, Roman Petre was confirmed as the president of the National Salvation Front, the party that holds power in Romania. Petre has presided over the country's post-Communist economic reforms.*
July- Aug. 1992	On July 29, **Erich Honecker** is flown to Berlin to face a trial for manslaughter, in connection with the "**shoot-to-kill**"policy of East German regime.			On July 17, President **Václav Havel** resigns, after the Slovak National Council adopts a sovereignty declaration. On August 26, Czech and Slovak leaders agree to divide Czechoslovakia on January 1, 1993.	
Sept.- Oct. 1992			On Sept. 4, **Todor Zhivkov** of Bulgaria is sentenced to seven years in prison for embezzlement. On October 11, **Ion Iliescu** of Romania is reelected president.		

Nov.-Dec. 1992	On November 20, **NATO** and the **European Union** impose a full naval blockade of **Yugoslavia** to enforce a U.N. embargo.		*In June 1992, Dubček ▶ (left), the chairman of Czechoslovakia's parliament, met with Vladimír Mečiar, the leader of Slovakia's separatist movement.*		

					Jan.-Feb. 1992
Wave of strikes protesting price increases sweeps Poland in January.		On January 15, Croatia is recognized by the **European Union** states. After a cease-fire negotiated in January, U.N. forces are deployed in special areas in February.		Macedonia declares independence in January and is recognized by **Bulgaria**. Slovenia is recognized by the **European Union** states.	
	On March 3, Bosnia and Herzegovina's president, **Alija Izetbegovič**, proclaims the republic's independence. By the end of April, more than 400,000 people are left homeless as a result of ethnic violence between Bosnian Serbs and Muslims.		On April 7, **Serbia** and **Montenegro** formally establish a new Yugoslavia. ◄ *In July 1992, Milan Panić (left), an American citizen, became prime minister of Yugoslavia.*	Macedonia and Slovenia establish diplomatic relations on March 17.	**March-April 1992**
	During May and June, **Sarajevo** is under intensive attack by Serbian irregulars, supported by the Yugoslav army. On June 29, U.N. troops take over the Sarajevo airport.		On May 30, U.N. imposes comprehensive sanctions against Yugoslavia. On June 28, about 100,000 demonstrators demand the ouster of **Slobodan Milošević**.		**May-June1 1992**
On July 8, Hanna Suchocka becomes Poland's premier, the first woman premier in the country's history and the fifth premier in the post-Communist period.	Fresh military offensives are launched by Serbian forces on July 13. In August, refugees claim that Serbs have established concentration camps in Serb-held northern Bosnia.	On August 2, **Franjo Tudjman** is reelected to the presidency in direct elections.	A Serbian-born U.S. citizen, Milan Panić, becomes prime minister of Yugoslavia on July 14. On August 13, U.N. security resolution condemns the Serbian policy of "**ethnic cleansing**."		**July-Aug. 1992**
			On September 22, Yugoslavia is expelled from the United Nations. ◄ *Reports of Serbian concentration camps in Bosnia and Herzegovina met with international condemnation. The U.N. also denounced the Serbian policy of "ethnic cleansing."*		**Sept.-Oct. 1992**
			On December 20, **Slobodan Milošević** is reelected to the presidency of **Serbia** by 56% of the vote. On December 29, the parliament ousts premier Milan Panić, after he is accused of being a foreign agent.		**Nov.-Dec. 1992**

57

	COMMONWEALTH OF INDEPENDENT STATES (CIS)	RUSSIA	UKRAINE	BELARUS MOLDOVA	ESTONIA LATVIA LITHUANIA
Jan.-Feb. 1992	**Price liberalization** is introduced in most CIS states in early January. Several coordination meetings are held in January and February concerning economic agreements and military affairs.	On January 29, **Boris Yeltsin** issues a decree on accelerating **privatization**. **Yeltsin** visits the **U.S.**, Canada, and France in February.	Ukraine and **Russia** debate the status of **Crimea**.	On January 16, Moldova establishes diplomatic relations with **Hungary**.	On January 25-26, the Interparliamentary Baltic Assembly holds its first meeting.
March-April 1992	On March 13, CIS members agree that an independent agency should administer the former **U.S.S.R.**'s foreign debt.	On March 30, a Federation Treaty is signed by 18 of **Russia**'s 20 autonomous republics. Chechen-Ingushetia and Tatarstan abstain.	On March 1, Ukraine introduces coupons as a new currency.	Fighting in the **Dnestr Republic** leads to the imposition of a state of emergency on March 28.	On March 9, Latvia signs an agreement on economic cooperation with **Russia**.
May-June 1992	On May 23, **U.S.** signs a treaty with **Russia**, **Ukraine**, **Belarus**, and **Kazakhstan** on strategic arms reduction.	On June 11, Russia launches the **privatization** of state enterprises.		On May 25, Belarus introduces a new currency called *rubel*. Fighting in **Dnestr Republic** continues in May and June.	
July-Aug. 1992	On August 3, **Boris Yeltsin** of Russia and Leonid Kravchuk of **Ukraine** reach an agreement on the Black Sea Fleet.	On July 1, the second stage of the "shock-therapy" economic reform program begins.		On July 7, a cease-fire in the **Dnestr Republic** is negotiated. The Moldovan parliament agrees to the deployment of Russian peace-keeping forces in the region.	Tension grows in the **Baltic Republics,** particularly in Estonia, over the continued presence of 130,000 foreign troops. Citizenship laws in Estonia and Latvia curb the rights of ethnic Russians.
Sept.-Oct. 1992			*Since its founding in December 1991, the Commonwealth of Independent States has helped coordinate trade and disarmament policies among the former Soviet republics.* ▼		In October, former Communists win Lithuania's first election since independence.
Nov.-Dec. 1992	On November 21, the first group of 100 **U.S.** Peace Corps volunteers arrives in Moscow, part of a wider Peace Corps program to help the former Soviet republics in their transition to democracy.	In early November, **Boris Yeltsin** imposes a state of emergency in north **Ossetia** and Ingushetia in an effort to stop ethnic fighting. At a meeting of the Congress of People's Deputies in early December, **Boris Yeltsin** survives a showdown with hard-liners.			

AZERBAIJAN ARMENIA	GEORGIA	KAZAKHSTAN KYRGYZSTAN	TAJIKISTAN TURKMENISTAN UZBEKISTAN	UNITED STATES AND OTHER COUNTRIES	
During January and February, fighting intensifies in **Nagorny Karabakh**. Armenian attack on the Azerbaijani-inhabited town of Khojali within Nagorny Karabakh on February 26–27 leaves hundreds dead.	Armed conflict between supporters and opponents of President Zviad Gamsakhurdia leads to the latter's deposition. A military council takes power and, on February 21, restores the constitution from 1921.	On February 24-25, some 17,000 conscripts demonstrate at the Baikonur space center in Kazakhstan in protest against poor living conditions.	On January 16, **price liberalization** leads to riots in Tashkent, Uzbekistan.	Mongolian parliament on January 13 adopts a constitution that renounces socialism and describes Mongolia as a republic with parliamentary government.	Jan.-Feb. 1992
On March 6, Azerbaijan's president Ayaz Mutalibov resigns, accused of failing to defend Azerbaijani lives in **Nagorny Karabakh**.	On March 10, **Eduard Shevardnadze** becomes head of the new State Council. Fighting continues in **Abkhazia** and South **Ossetia**.			◄ *In May 1992, Nursultan Nazarbayev, Kazakhstan's president, met with U.S. President George Bush.*	March-April 1992
On June 7, a staunch nationalist, Abulfaz Elchibey, is elected president of Azerbaijan. He vows never to give up **Nagorny Karabakh**.	On June 24, an agreement between Georgia and **Russia** leads to the stationing of a peacekeeping force in **Ossetia**.	In early May, Kazakhstan concludes a $10 billion deal with Chevron to develop the Tenghiz oil fields.	Anti-Communist demonstrations in Tajikistan lead to the creation of a coalition government on May 12.	On June 28, ex-Communists win in elections in Mongolia.	May-June 1992
	Fighting in **Abkhazia** on August 25-26 results in dozens of deaths.				July-Aug. 1992
			◄ *In October 1992, Eduard Shevardnadze, formerly the foreign minister of the Soviet Union, became the Speaker of the Parliament for the republic of Georgia.*		
			On September 7, Tajikistan's president **Rakhman Nabiyev** is seized by opposition militiamen and forced to resign.	At its 14th congress, the Chinese Communist Party reasserts strict party control in politics, but confirms its support for a free-market economy.	Sept.-Oct. 1992
On November 9, the Azerbaijani air force attacks Stepanakert, the capital of **Nagorny Karabakh**.	On November 11, **Eduard Shevardnadze** inspects **Abkhazia**, a region of Georgia troubled by ethnic strife.		In November, the Islamic-led coalition government of Tajikistan is overthrown and a pro-Moscow regime is installed.	On November 3, **Bill Clinton** wins the presidential election in the **United States**.	Nov.-Dec. 1992

Jan.-Feb. 1993

On Jan. 1, **Czechoslovakia** splits into the Czech Republic and Slovakia.

On Jan. 26, **Václav Havel** is elected president of the Czech Republic.

On Feb. 15, Michal Kováč is elected president of Slovakia.

March-April 1993

In April, **John Paul II** visits Albania, the first-ever papal visit to the country.

▲
The split of Czechoslovakia into the Czech Republic and Slovakia (map above) was accompanied by much ceremony, especially in Bratislava, the Slovakian capital. The euphoria has all but disappeared in the intervening years.

May-June 1993

On May 28, Denmark ratifies the **Maastricht Treaty**.

In late June, large anti-government demonstrations take place in Bulgaria, protesting against government interference with the media and the slowing down of economic reform.

July- Aug. 1993

On July 23, Britain ratifies the **Maastricht Treaty**.

In August, miners in Romania protest against low wages and high prices.

Sept.- Oct. 1993

On Oct. 11, **Germany** ratifies the **Maastricht Treaty**; it is the last country to do so.

On Oct. 20-21, **NATO** offers the **Partnership for Peace** program to former Communist countries.

◀ *In 1993, the historic bridge at Mostar, the provincial capital of Herzegovina, was severely damaged by Bosnian Croats. The bridge, built in 1566, was a superb example of Ottoman architecture.*

Nov.-Dec. 1993

On Nov. 1, the **Maastricht Treaty** takes effect, creating the **European Union**.

On Dec. 12, Prime Minister Jozsef Antall dies; he had been in office since 1990.

On Feb. 2, in Geneva, a conference presided over by Cyrus Vance and Lord Owen studies ways to end the war in Bosnia and Herzegovina.

In February, the **United States** begins parachuting humanitarian aid to Muslim-held parts of Bosnia.

◄ *Each side in the fighting in Bosnia and Herzegovina has taken its share of prisoners. In October 1993, the Red Cross negotiated the release of some 1,000 prisoners of war.*

On Apr. 15, fighting between Bosnian Croats and Serbs begins.

On April 8, Macedonia joins the United Nations under the provisional name of "The Former Yugoslav Republic of Macedonia."

On May 7, in an important **privatization** act, the Parliament agrees to transfer control of 600 state enterprises to investment funds, with shares in the funds to be distributed to Polish citizens.

On May 28, Hanna Suchocka resigns from the premiership.

On May 6, the Bosnian-Serb parliament rejects the U.N. Vance-Owen peace plan; on May 15-16, the Bosnian Serbs follow suit in a referendum.

On June 6, the U.N. Security Council establishes six "safe areas": Srebrenica Goražde, Tuzla, Zepa, Bihać, and **Sarajevo**.

On June 19-20, in a referendum in Serbian-held Krajina, 98.6% of voters say "yes" to a union with Bosnian Serbs and "other Serb states."

On June 1, moderate president Dobrica Cosić is voted out of office by the parliament, at the urging of **Slobodan Milošević**.

On June 18, eight military officers come to Macedonia to plan the deployment of United Nations force.

In Belgrade, the capital of Yugoslavia, residents ▶ scramble to receive free milk being dispensed by an antigovernment party. The ongoing conflict and international sanctions contributed to a severe lack of basic food products.

On Sept. 18, the last Russian soldiers leave Poland.

On Sept. 19, former Communists and other left-wing parties win in parliamentary elections.

On Oct. 26, Waldemar Pawlak becomes the new prime minister.

On Oct. 4, the U.N. Security Council extends the mandate of its 14,000 troops in Croatia by another six months.

On Nov. 9, Bosnian Croats almost completely destroy the historic bridge in Mostar.

In the Dec. 19 general elections, **Slobodan Milošević's** Serbian Socialist Party wins 123 out of 250 seats in the parliament.

In December, most **European Union** countries announce plans to recognize Macedonia.

	COMMONWEALTH OF INDEPENDENT STATES (CIS)	RUSSIA	UKRAINE	BELARUS MOLDOVA	ESTONIA LITHUANIA LATVIA
Jan.-Feb 1993				In February, Belarus ratifies the START I treaty.	On Feb. 14, a former Communist, Algirdas Brazauskas, wins in the presidential elections in Lithuania.
March-April 1993		On March 28, a vote to impeach **Boris Yeltsin** fails by just 72 votes. On Apr. 2, the creditor nations agree to reschedule about 75% of the $20-billion debt payments that Russia should pay in 1993. In a referendum on Apr. 25, 58.7% of the voters express confidence in **Yeltsin**.			
May-June 1993					On June 5-6, the first post-Soviet parliamentary elections take place in Latvia; the winners are former Communists and some émigrés.
July-Aug. 1993		On July 9, seven Western industrialized nations (G7) announce a $3 billion loan package to Russia.	In August, the Ukrainian currency collapses in a free fall.	On Aug. 5, the Moldovan parliament refuses to ratify a monetary union accord with the **CIS**.	On Aug. 31, the last Russian troops withdraw from Lithuania.
Sept.-Oct 1993	In September, **Azerbaijan** and **Georgia** request membership in the CIS. On Sept. 24, nine CIS republics establish an economic union.	On Sept. 21, **Yeltsin** dissolves the Russian parliament. A bloody confrontation between **Yeltsin** and the "White House" parliament in early October results in 187 deaths. A state of emergency is declared on Oct. 3.	On Sept. 22, Prime Minister Leonid Kuchma resigns after his proposed economic reform package is not endorsed by the parliament.		
Nov.-Dec 1993	In December, the CIS states decline **Yeltsin**'s request for special status for Russians living in their territories.	On Dec. 11, 60% of voters approve a new Russian constitution. The strongest party in parliamentary elections on the same date are ultranationalists and neoimperialists led by Vladimír Zhirinovsky, who receive 23% of the vote. Ironically, the party is called Liberal Democrats.		In November, Moldova introduces a new currency called the "leu."	

▲
By 1993, many Russians had begun to wonder whether the abandonment of Communism had been a good idea. Some of these dissatisfied people began to support former Communists or ultranationalists like Vladimir Zhirinovsky (above).

A government of former Communists is installed in Tajikistan in January.

On Jan. 3, **Russia** and the United States sign the START II arms treaty.

Jan.-Feb. 1993

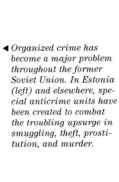

◄ *Organized crime has become a major problem throughout the former Soviet Union. In Estonia (left) and elsewhere, special anticrime units have been created to combat the troubling upsurge in smuggling, theft, prostitution, and murder.*

March-April 1993

On June 30, the pro-Turkish Abulfez Elchibey is ousted from the presidency of Azerbaijan and replaced by a former Communist, Geidar Aliyev.

In May, Kyrgyzstan introduces its own currency, called the "som," and withdraws from the **CIS** ruble zone.

May-June 1993

In late July, a ceasefire is signed in **Nagorny Karabakh**.

On July 6, martial law is declared in **Abkhazia**; then, under pressure from **Russia**, a cease-fire takes effect on July 27.

In July, great floods devastate parts of the U.S. Midwest.

July-Aug. 1993

On. Oct. 10, Geidar Aliyev receives almost 99% in presidential elections in Azerbaijan.

On Sept. 27, rebels in **Abkhazia** capture the province's capital of Sukhumi; Georgia's president, **Eduard Shevardnadze**, flees at the last minute.

In 1993, domestic ▶ issues and local disasters caused the United States government to focus more on problems at home than on crises abroad.

Sept.-Oct 1993

In December, Azerbaijan undertakes a counteroffensive against Armenia.

On Dec. 1, the government of Georgia signs peace accord with **Abkhazia**, on the basis of U.N.-sponsored talks on political settlement.

On Dec. 31, the former president of Georgia, Zviad Gamsakhurdia, reportedly commits suicide.

At the beginning of November, Turkmenistan introduces its own currency, called the "manat."

Nov.-Dec 1993

63

Jan.-Feb. 1994

◄ *In January 1994, U.S. President Bill Clinton met with Czech President Václav Havel in Prague. The topics discussed included new security arrangements in Eastern Europe.*

March-April 1994

On Apr. 4, Fatos Nano, a former prime minister of Albania and leader of the main opposition Socialist Party, is sentenced to 12 years in prison. His popularity apparently irritated the increasingly authoritarian president, **Sali Berisha**.

In early March, **Vladimír Mečiar** of Slovakia loses a vote of confidence and steps down as prime minister. He is replaced by Jozef Moravšík.

◄ *Vladimír Mečiar was ousted as prime minister of Slovakia in March 1994, after his government suffered a vote of no confidence. Mečiar returned to power in October.*

May-June 1994

On May 6, the 31-mile-long English Channel tunnel is inaugurated.

On June 12, voters in Austria endorse their country's accession to the European Union by a 2 to 1 margin.

On May 29, the Socialist Party (former Communists) wins parliamentary elections; Gyula Horn becomes prime minister.

July-Aug. 1994

The fall of Communism has brought a religious revival to Albania. The Muslims below are praying at a mosque in Tirana, the capital of Albania. ▼

Sept.-Oct. 1994

On Sept. 30-Oct. 1, **Vladimír Mečiar**'s party, the Movement for Democratic Slovakia, wins in extraordinary elections, and Mečiar again becomes prime minister.

Nov.-Dec. 1994

In November, 52% of voters in Sweden agree to join the European Union.

On Dec. 18, the Bulgarian Socialist Party (former Communists) wins parliamentary elections and gains a majority of the seats in the parliament.

In November, communal elections take place in the Czech Republic; the Civic Democratic Party led by **Václav Klaus** wins.

On Feb. 9, 25,000 **Solidarity** members demonstrate against the government.

On Feb. 5, 68 people are killed by a mortar in Sarajevo's market.

On Feb. 9, **NATO** threatens air strikes; on Feb. 17, Bosnian Serbs withdraw heavy weapons from around **Sarajevo**.

On Feb. 28, **NATO** shoots down four Serb aircraft.

In February, both **Russia** and the **United States** recognize Macedonia.

◄ *Jets aboard the U.S.S. Saratoga (left) prepare to confront Bosnian Serb ground-attack jets in the U.N.-imposed no-fly zone.*

Jan.-Feb. 1994

On March 18, Bosnian Croats and Muslims agree to form a federation.

On April 10 and 11, **NATO** planes bomb Bosnian Serbian targets.

On April 15, Bosnian Serbs attack Goražde, a U.N. "safe area."

On April 27, Bosnian Serbs obey **NATO**'s pullout order from Goražde.

On March 30, a cease-fire is signed in the Serb-held eastern region of Croatia called Krajina.

In March, Slovenia's leading party, the Liberal Democratic Party, merges with three smaller parties and renames itself the Liberal Democracy of Slovenia.

March-April 1994

On May 31, the new Muslim-Croatian alliance elects a president.

In February 1994, a Serb ► mortar attack on a crowded open-air market in Sarajevo left 68 civilians dead.

May-June 1994

On August 7, attacks on **Sarajevo** resume.

On August 4, Yugoslavia cuts ties to the Bosnian Serbs.

July-Aug.1994

On Sept. 23, the U.N. votes for a conditional easing of sanctions against Yugoslavia.

Sept.-Oct. 1994

Nov.-Dec. 1994

65

	COMMONWEALTH OF INDEPENDENT STATES (CIS)	RUSSIA	UKRAINE	BELARUS MOLDOVA	ESTONIA LITHUANIA LATVIA
Jan.-Feb. 1994		On Jan. 14, in a TV speech, President **Bill Clinton** urges Russians to press for democracy. On Jan. 16, several high officials resign, charging that the reform process is being halted. On Feb. 23, the parliament frees leaders of the October 1993 challenge to President **Boris Yeltsin**.	On Feb. 2, the Ukrainian parliament ratifies the Jan. 14 agreement with **Russia** and the **United States** to scrap atomic weapons.	**Bill Clinton** visits Belarus on Jan. 15 and promises $15 million in additional help. In February, the former Communist establishment wins in Moldova and **Mircea Snegur** is reelected president.	
March-April 1994	On March 1, **Georgia** joins the CIS.	On April 20, International Monetary Fund approves a $1.5 billion loan to Russia.	On Apr. 10, the Communists and their allies win in general elections.	In a plebiscite on March 6, Moldova's electorate rejects reunification with **Romania**. In April, Belarus and **Russia** sign a monetary and customs-union treaty.	
May-June 1994		On June 22, Russia becomes the 21st nation to join the **Partnership for Peace** program.		▲ *In 1994, Ukrainians cast ballots in several elections. In July, they selected Leonid Kuchma, the former head of the U.S.S.R.'s largest missile factory, as president.*	
July-Aug. 1994		On Aug. 31, Russian troops leave Berlin, after 49 years.	On July 10, Leonid Kuchma becomes president of Ukraine.	On July 11, Aleksandr Lukashenko becomes the first president of Belarus, after receiving 80% of the votes.	On Aug. 31, the last Russian troops leave Estonia and Latvia, ending a presence of 54 years.
Sept.-Oct. 1994		In October, the ruble collapses.			
Nov.-Dec. 1994		On Dec. 11, Russian troops are sent into **Chechnya**. *The arrival of Russian ▶ troops in the breakaway republic of Chechnya in late 1994 began more than six months of brutal fighting*			

AZERBAIJAN ARMENIA	GEORGIA	KAZAKHSTAN KYRGYZSTAN	TAJIKISTAN TURKMENISTAN UZBEKISTAN	UNITED STATES AND OTHER COUNTRIES	
	On. Feb. 3, Georgia signs a military cooperation treaty with **Russia**.	On Feb. 14, Kazakhstan agrees to dismantle its nuclear missiles.	In February, 99.99% of Turkmenistan's voters agree to extend President Saparmurat Niyazov's term of office until 1999.	On Feb. 9, President **Bill Clinton** ends the trade embargo against Vietnam.	Jan.-Feb. 1994
	In October 1994, Queen Elizabeth II ▶ became the first British monarch to visit Russia. During her four-day tour of Moscow and St. Petersburg, she inspected Russian landmarks and held talks with Boris Yeltsin (at right). 	General elections take place on March 7 in Kazakhstan; they are later declared illegal.			March-April 1994
In May, a temporary cease-fire is announced in **Nagorny Karabakh**, with Armenian forces in control.	On May 14, a cease-fire agreement is signed with **Abkhazia**'s rebels, providing for Russian peacekeepers.			On May 4, Israel and Palestinians sign an accord on Israeli withdrawal from the West Bank.	May-June 1994
				On July 6, Kim Il Sung of North Korea, the longest-ruling Communist leader, dies after 49 years in power.	July-Aug. 1994
On Sept. 20, a "contract of the century" is signed by an international consortium in Baku about the exploitation of Azerbaijan's oil. An attempted coup in Azerbaijan is crushed in October; a state of emergency is declared.		In September, President Askar Akayev of Kyrgyzstan dissolves parliament.	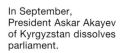 *After 49 years in power, North Korea's President Kim Il Sung died in 1994. Hundreds of thousands mourners attended a memorial service for him two weeks after his death.* ◀	On Sept. 8, last U.S., French, and British troops leave Berlin.	Sept.-Oct. 1994
In December, the president of Armenia bans Dashnak, the best-known opposition party.			On Nov. 6, Imamali Rakhmonov is confirmed president of Tajikistan in rigged elections. On Dec. 25, elections take place in Uzbekistan; the People's Democratic Party (former Communists), wins overwhelmingly.		Nov.-Dec. 1994

67

Jan.-Feb. 1995

March-April 1995

In March, the government presents a radical reform package to cut public-sector spending. Two-thirds of Hungarians are strongly opposed to it.

May-June 1995

On June 19, **Arpad Göncz** is reelected to the presidency for another five-year term.

On Aug. 31, the son of President Michal Kováč of Slovakia is kidnapped.

July-Aug. 1995

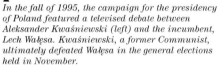

▲ *In the fall of 1995, the campaign for the presidency of Poland featured a televised debate between Aleksander Kwaśniewski (left) and the incumbent, Lech Wałęsa. Kwaśniewski, a former Communist, ultimately defeated Wałęsa in the general elections held in November.*

Sept.-Oct. 1995

On Sept. 22-23, the European Union heads of government meet in Majorca to prepare for the Intergovernmental Conference (IGC), which should work out the procedure for the accession of ex-Communist countries to EU.

On Sept. 23, the parliament passes a law on "genocide and communist crimes," which bars thousands of former Communist officials from serving in public office until 2002.

▲ *The ethnic wars that have swept across the area that was formerly Yugoslavia have created innumerable refugees. Above, ethnic Croats flee across the Sava River to safety in Davor, Croatia.*

On Oct. 25, the **EU** expresses serious concerns about the escalating conflict between Slovakia's president, Michal Kováč, and Prime Minister **Vladimír Mečiar**.

Nov.-Dec. 1995

In December, the European Union summit takes place in Madrid.

On Nov. 1, doctors in state clinics and polyclinics in the Czech Republic begin an "administrative strike," protesting low salaries and lack of reform in the public-health sector.

On Feb. 7, Prime Minister Pawlak resigns.	A cease-fire takes effect on Jan. 1.				Jan.-Feb. 1995
	In December 1995, American troops began arriving in Bosnia and Herzegovina to help monitor the implementation of the peace accords negotiated in Dayton, Ohio, by the various warring factions in the former Yugoslavia. ▶				March-April 1995
	On May 25 and 26, **NATO** planes at the behest of the U.N. bomb Bosnian Serb ammunition plants. Serbs retaliate by shelling the "safe area" of Tuzla and by taking about 370 U.N. troops as hostages. They also shoot down a **U.S.** F-16 plane.	On May 1 and 2, Croatian army captures Western Slavonia, the most vulnerable part of Serbian-held Krajina.			May-June 1995
	On July 11, the "safe area" of Srebrenica falls into Serbian hands. Zepa is conquered shortly thereafter. On Aug. 28, Bosnian Serbs shell a market in **Sarajevo**, killing 37 people. On Aug. 30, **NATO** launches its most massive military operation ever, in three days sending 250 planes to bomb Serbian targets.	On Aug. 4-6, in a massive offensive, the Croatian army takes control of Krajina, which had been held by the Serbs since 1992.	In early August, at least 150,000—and possibly 200,000—Serbian refugees flee from Krajina in **Croatia** to Yugoslavia.		July-Aug. 1995
	In September, Croats help Bosnian Muslims to recapture more than 1,500 square miles from the Bosnian Serbs. On. Oct. 12, a cease-fire is proclaimed.	In Oct. 29 elections, President **Tudjman**'s party, the Democratic Union, wins 45% of the vote.		On Oct. 3, an unsuccessful assassination attempt at Macedonia's president, Kiro Gligorov, takes place.	Sept.-Oct. 1995
On Nov. 5, in the first round of presidential elections, the winner is a former Communist, Aleksander Kwaśniewski, with 34% of the vote. The runner up is **Lech Wałęsa**, with 31%. On Nov. 19, Kwasniewski wins in the second round of presidential elections.	In early November, the presidents of Bosnia and Herzegovina, **Croatia** and **Yugoslavia** meet in Dayton, Ohio, to negotiate an end the war in Bosnia and Herzegovina. On Dec. 14, a peace accord is signed in Paris.	On Nov. 12, the peace talks in Dayton, Ohio, lead to the return of Serb-occupied Eastern Slavonia to Croatian administration.			Nov.-Dec. 1995

69

	COMMONWEALTH OF INDEPENDENT STATES (CIS)	RUSSIA	UKRAINE	BELARUS MOLDOVA	ESTONIA LITHUANIA LATVIA
Jan.-Feb. 1995	On Feb. 11, 12 member states meet in Alma Ata in **Kazakhstan**. **Belarus** and Kazakhstan are eager to strengthen their ties with **Russia** by creating a customs union.	In January, Russian forces advance in **Chechnya**; in late January, they take the presidential palace in Grozny.			
March-April 1995			On March 17, Ukraine's parliament annuls **Crimea**'s constitution.	In April, Prime Minister Lukashenko of Belarus dissolves parliament.	In March, former Communists win in parliamentary elections in Estonia.
May-June 1995		On June 14, 200 Chechen suicide commandos attack the Russian city of Budyonnovsk, taking more than 1,000 hostages and holding them in a hospital. Russian troops storm the hospital, killing many hostages. Prime minister Chernomyrdin then negotiates a cease-fire. On June 21, **Yeltsin** receives a no-confidence vote because of Budyonnovsk. To avoid a second no-confidence vote, Yeltsin sacks the three ministers responsible for the affair.	In late May, Ukraine obtains a $2.5 billion loan from the International Monetary Fund.	On May 15, 80% of voters in Belarus agree in a referendum to make Russian a state language and to create an "economic integration" with Russia.	
July-Aug. 1995		On July 30, an agreement is signed by Russians and Chechens to settle their conflict by negotiations.			
Sept.-Oct. 1995					On Oct. 1, the two strongest parties in parliamentary elections in Latvia are the former Communists (Saimniek) and anti-Russian fascists.
Nov.-Dec. 1995		On Dec. 17, Communists win in parliamentary elections in Russia.			

▲
Campaign rallies have become part of the political scene in Russia. Above, members of the Liberal Democratic Party greet party leader Vladimír Zhirinovsky at a rally in December 1995. In the parliamentary elections held later that month, Zhirinovsky's party lost to the Communists.

AZERBAIJAN ARMENIA	GEORGIA	KAZAKHSTAN KYRGYZSTAN	TAJIKISTAN TURKMENISTAN UZBEKISTAN	UNITED STATES AND OTHER COUNTRIES	
		In January, **Russia** and Kazakhstan agree to tighten economic and military links.			Jan.-Feb. 1995
On March 17, the Azerbaijani government crushes an armed rebellion, and the state of emergency is extended.	In March, Georgia signs an agreement that allows **Russia** to keep military bases in Georgia for 25 years.	On March 11, President **Nazarbayev** of Kazakhstan dissolves parliament.	On March 26, 99.96% of the voters in Uzbekistan agree to extend president **Islam Karimov**'s term of office until 2000.		March-April 1995
		On April 29, 95% of voters in Kazakhstan agree to extend the president's term of office until 2000.			May-June 1995

▲
U.S. President Bill Clinton speaks at the signing ceremony for the Bosnian peace accords, held in Paris on December 14, 1995. The Clinton Administration had played a prominent role in getting the warring factions to the negotiating table.

AZERBAIJAN ARMENIA	GEORGIA	KAZAKHSTAN KYRGYZSTAN	TAJIKISTAN TURKMENISTAN UZBEKISTAN	UNITED STATES AND OTHER COUNTRIES	
	On Aug. 29, President **Eduard Shevardnadze** barely escapes an assassination attempt.				July-Aug. 1995
					Sept.-Oct. 1995
On Nov. 12, parliamentary elections take place in Azerbaijan, and the president's party wins. According to observers, there are many irregularities.				On Nov. 4, Yitzhak Rabin of Israel is assassinated. In Dec. U.S. troops arrive in **Bosnia and Herzegovina**.	Nov.-Dec. 1995

71

As the 20th century draws to a close, representatives of the countries that comprise the European Union continue to meet on a regular basis to formulate plans toward creating a united Europe.

THE CHANGING FACE OF EUROPE:
An Alphabetical Overview

ABKHAZIA, a small region in northwest **Georgia** on the Black Sea, has a 100,000-strong separatist Turkic-speaking minority that, in the early 1990s, fought for independence from Georgia with the help of Russian mercenaries. **Russia** arranged a cease-fire in May 1994, but a stalemate persists.

ALBANIA, a mountainous Alabama-sized country on the Balkan Peninsula, is the poorest nation in Europe. Albania has a population of 3.4 million; another 2 million Albanians live outside the country, mostly in the Serbian province of **Kosovo** and in **Macedonia**.

Despite centuries of foreign rule, Albanians have preserved a separate identity. The country gained political independence in 1920, but during World War II was annexed by Italy. Communist guerrillas fought the Italian and German forces and, in 1944, a Communist government led by Enver Hoxha was established.

Professing a fierce self-reliance, Albania first broke with the **U.S.S.R.** and later with China. The government prohibited any borrowing from the West; by the end of the 1970s, the country was almost entirely isolated internationally. Its Communist leaders, claiming that Albania was the only state truly following the precepts of **Marxism-Leninism**, prepared for the onslaught of its enemies by building 320,000 concrete bunkers that now cover the entire countryside.

The tremors shaking the Communist world began to reach Albania in early 1990. Enver Hoxha's successor, Ramiz Alia, announced a program of "democratization," allowing farmers to cultivate private plots, making foreign travel more accessible, and permitting Albanians to practice religious rites in the privacy of their homes. Although Alia tried to stay in power as a reformist, the historical process swept him away. The first multiparty elections took place in the spring of 1991; in the next national elections, in March 1992, the opposition Democratic Party won a landslide victory. A month later, **Sali Berisha** became Albania's first non-Communist president.

Meanwhile, the country was being overwhelmed by strikes, riots, and looting. Old vendettas reemerged, and economic and social chaos became almost uncontrollable. Tens of thousands of Albanians left the country in search of a better future. The economic situation stabilized somewhat in 1993, but the country remains extraordinarily backward and poor.

During 1992 and 1993, several former Communist officials were sentenced to prison terms, mostly for abuse of power and corruption. The ruling Democratic Party has become quite intolerant of any political opposition.

ARMENIA, a landlocked, mountainous republic in the **Caucasus**, is slightly larger than Maryland. It has a population of about 3.7 million people.

One of the earliest centers of civilization, Armenia was the first country to adopt Christianity as a state religion (in the 4th century). For much of its history, periods of independence alternated with periods of foreign rule (by Turkey and Persia), until in the early 19th century, Armenia became part of the Russian Empire.

During the Communist era, the country slumbered in the gray uniformity of Soviet life. Since the late 1980s, however, it has been embroiled in a violent ethnic conflict over a region called **Nagorny Karabakh**, which lies within **Azerbaijan** but is inhabited mostly by Armenians. This province has historical significance for both countries. The hostility feeds on the religious, ethnic, and economic disparities between the Christian, Indo-European, and generally more affluent Armenians and the Muslim, Turkic, and poorer Azerbaijanis. In 1993, Armenia seized large parts of Azerbaijan's territory, an action condemned by the United Nations. In retaliation, Azerbaijan and Turkey cut off energy supplies, depriving Armenians of heat and lighting for long periods, and leading to the emigration of perhaps half a million people.

By 1995, Armenia's prospects had begun to improve. Supported by a large diaspora, mostly in the United States, the country seems on its way to economic recovery. Although president **Levon Ter-Petrosyan** remains the only post-Soviet leader without a Communist past, he rather undemocratically cracked down on opposition in December 1994.

AZERBAIJAN, until 1991 a Soviet republic in the **Caucasus**, is inhabited by a predominantly Muslim population of 7.4 million. The region was ruled by Islamic dynasties from the 7th century until the early 19th century, when it became part of the Russian Empire.

Since 1988, Azerbaijan has fought an undeclared war with **Armenia** over a small region within its territory called **Nagorny Karabakh**. The conflict escalated in early 1992; in May of that year, Armenia also launched a full-scale attack on the Azerbaijani province of Nakhichevan, a small region sandwiched between Armenia and Iran. In June, a staunch nationalist and a former opponent of Communism, Abulfaz Elchibey, was

Ethnic conflicts have erupted in many of the republics that formerly made up the Soviet Union. The strife between Armenia and Azerbaijan has been particularly bitter.

elected president of Azerbaijan, and the country then left the **Commonwealth of Independent States (CIS)**. The following year, however, the anti-Russian and pro-Turkish Elchibey was ousted from power and replaced by a former Communist, Geidar Aliyev. Azerbaijan rejoined the CIS in late 1993.

By 1995, the undeclared war with Armenia had driven about 1 million Azerbaijanis from their homes and destroyed much of the country's economy. There might be a brighter future ahead, however, thanks to Azerbaijan's huge oil reserves. The government and an international consortium signed a "contract of the century" for oil exploitation in September 1994, with U.S. and British companies owning the largest share. Another contract was signed in November 1995, giving a Russian firm 32.5 percent of the capital. Geidar Aliyev, who had once been a sycophantic follower of **Brezhnev**, now goes on visits to Arab countries, promising to transform Azerbaijan into a "new Kuwait."

BALTIC REPUBLICS are three former Soviet republics—**Lithuania, Latvia,** and **Estonia**—that were forcibly integrated into the **U.S.S.R.** in 1940–41, on the basis of secret protocols appended to the Soviet-Nazi pact of 1939. All three republics seceded from the U.S.S.R. in September 1991. Since then they have been working hard to shake off Russian influence— a more difficult process than most had imagined. A dispute with **Russia** over the 130,000 ex-Soviet military personnel stationed in Baltic territory finally ended in August 1994 when their withdrawal was completed.

Thanks mostly to help from the Scandinavian countries, Estonia has performed best in its economic transformation. The pain of transition, however, left voters disappointed and led to the victories of former Communists in all three republics.

BELARUS was the third-largest republic of the **U.S.S.R.**; until it gained independence in late 1991, it was referred to in Western sources as Belorussia or Byelorussia. The country, a bit smaller than Kansas, has a population of 10.3 million.

Belarus is a founding member of the **Commonwealth of Independent States**. Belorussians have never felt a strong separate national identity and the country remains tied to Russia in countless ways; in fact, most of the people speak Russian rather than Belorussian as their everyday language. The pro-Russian president, Aleksandr Lukashenko, is not interested in any real economic or political reform.

BERISHA, SALI (1945–), a heart surgeon and former minor Communist apparatchik, became the first non-Communist president of **Albania** in April 1992. He prudently avoided inciting nationalist feelings of Albanians living in **Serbia** and **Macedonia**, although he has turned quite authoritarian.

BERLIN WALL was a leading symbol of the **Cold War**. At the end of World War II, Berlin was partitioned into four sectors: three under the

After much negotiation, the last of the Russian troops stationed in the Baltic Republics finally shipped out of Estonia and Latvia on August 31, 1994.

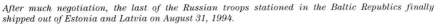

Western Allies and one under the **U.S.S.R.** After the creation of the Federal Republic of **Germany** and the German Democratic Republic in 1949, Berlin remained divided, but represented a major crack in the **Iron Curtain**. In August 1961, to prevent East Germans from fleeing to West Germany, the East German government erected an imposing 5-foot-tall concrete wall, topped with broken glass and barbed wire.

On November 9, 1989, after thousands of East Germans flooded the West German embassies in Prague and in Warsaw, the beleaguered East German leadership decided to open the borders. Within a few days, millions of East Germans crossed into West Berlin. By the end of 1990, the wall had been completely dismantled.

For 28 years, the Berlin Wall divided Communist East Berlin from capitalist West Berlin. West Berliners sometimes gathered at the wall to taunt the East German soldiers.

BOSNIA AND HERZEGOVINA experienced, from 1992 to 1995, the worst fighting in Europe since World War II. A former republic of **Yugoslavia**, Bosnia and Herzegovina is a landlocked Balkan country about the size of New Hampshire and Vermont combined. Its population in 1991 was 4.5 million, of which 44 percent were Muslims (ethnic Slavs who accepted Islam centuries ago), 31 percent Eastern Orthodox Serbs, and the rest Roman Catholic Croats. Throughout the Communist era, these three groups lived side by side in hundreds of mixed neighborhoods, villages, and towns—despite the historical animosities.

Bosnia and Herzegovina declared independence in March 1992; in April, Bosnian Serbs rose in armed conflict. The fighting spread and continued, with brief interruptions, until fall 1995, when the presidents of Bosnia and Herzegovina, **Croatia**, and **Serbia**, prodded by Americans, reached an agreement in Dayton, Ohio.

In August 1990, the Bulgarian parliament chose Zhelyu Zhelev, one of the country's few dissidents during the Communist period, to become president, a post he still retains.

BRANDT, WILLY (1913–92), was the chancellor of West **Germany** from 1969 to 1974. In 1971, he received the Nobel Peace Prize for his policy of opening to the East (the *Ostpolitik*). He was the chief advocate of **détente** and the main architect of the so-called Basic Treaties signed between the two Germanies in 1972.

BREZHNEV, LEONID (1906–85), was first secretary of the Communist Party of the **U.S.S.R.** from 1964 until his death in 1985. A colorless bureaucrat, Brezhnev concentrated on maintaining the status quo; the years of his rule were ultimately labeled the "period of stagnation." Ironically, it was during the 1970s that the U.S.S.R. seemed at the pinnacle of its power, with its influence reaching out in all directions.

BRUSSELS is the capital of Belgium and the seat of the governing bodies of the **European Union**. The city's name has become synonymous with the complex bureaucracy of the European Union.

BULGARIA, a hilly, Tennessee-sized Balkan country on the Black Sea, has a population of 8.4 million; its capital, Sofia, was founded by Romans in the 2nd century A.D. Bulgarians are the descendants of a mixture of Slavs and central Asian Turkic tribes of Bulgars, who invaded the Balkans in the 7th century. The early Bulgarian state adopted Christianity in the 9th century, then came under foreign rule; it rose again in the 12th and 13th centuries, but subsequently was conquered by Ottoman Turks. In 1878, Bulgaria gained independence thanks to Russian pressure on the Ottomans; Bulgarians have had friendly feelings toward Russia ever since.

Bulgaria became Communist in 1944, and its party leadership remained unquestionably loyal to Moscow until 1989; opposition to Communist rule was almost nonexistent. In October 1989, a few **dissident** groups held their first rallies while an international conference on the environment took place in Sofia. On November 10, the second-longest-ruling Eastern European leader, **Todor Zhivkov**, was forced to resign his office.

The non-Communist Union of Democratic Forces (UDF), in power in 1991 and 1992, was succeeded by a caretaker government. The former Communists, now calling themselves the Bulgarian Socialist Party, won in elections held in December 1994. The country is now more free and open than during the Communist era, but there have been few economic reforms. Bulgaria lags in **privatization** and **restitutions**, particularly of land. The non-Communist president, **Zhelyu Zhelev**, has little political power, yet his moral stature represents a guarantee of democracy.

In his one term, U.S. President George Bush (right) presided over the disintegration of the Soviet Union and met with Russia's first freely elected president, Boris Yeltsin.

BUSH, GEORGE (1924–), the forty-first president of the **United States** (1989–93), initially treated the changes in the **U.S.S.R.** and in **Eastern Europe** with caution. By late 1990, however, he had realized that an era was ending. At the meeting of the **Conference on Security and Cooperation in Europe**, Bush declared that the **Cold War** was over.

CAUCASUS is a mountainous region between the Black Sea and the Caspian Sea that straddles the border between Asia and Europe. It is inhabited by 22 larger and many smaller ethnic groups, most of them Muslim, which have often been at war with each other. Since the late 1980s, the area has seen many violent conflicts: between **Azerbaijan** and **Armenia**; in **Georgia**, particularly in its provinces of **Abkhazia** and **Ossetia**; and, in 1994 and 1995, in **Chechnya**, which is part of **Russia**. The highlanders of Caucasus are proud, fierce people known for their longevity. Moscow's dominance over the region, dating from the 19th century, has often had a pacifying effect; nonetheless, the peoples of the Caucasus have bitterly resented it.

CEAUŞESCU, NICOLAE (1918–89), was the general secretary of the Communist Party of **Romania** from 1965 until his death. Ceauşescu began as a nationalist who won admiration for his defiance of the **U.S.S.R.** in matters of foreign policy. He condemned the invasion of **Czechoslovakia** in 1968 and, in the early 1970s, became a frequent visitor to Western capitals.

Gradually, however, Ceauşescu turned into a megalomaniacal dictator. His 1982 decision to pay off all foreign debt plunged the country into darkness, and yet he began to build in downtown Bucharest a mammoth marble-covered palace, with thousands of rooms and such extravaganzas as a 980-bulb chandelier. While the Romanian people shivered in their unheated apartments, Ceauşescu devoted time every Sunday to pestering architects at the building site of the grandiose structure.

The dramatic demise of Ceauşescu was seen by millions of television viewers around the world: his utter disbelief when he was heckled during an official rally on December 20, 1989; his defiance at the hastily arranged trial several days later; and then his crumpled body minutes after his execution on December 25.

CHARTER 77 was the name of a manifesto issued by a group of 242 Czech and Slovak **dissidents** in early January 1977; among its first signatories was the future president of **Czechoslovakia**, **Václav Havel**. The manifesto, which in cautious language listed basic human-rights demands, provoked a furious backlash from the authorities. Signatories were arrested, forced into exile, or otherwise harassed; nonetheless, the core group formed at that time became the nucleus of the Czechoslovak dissident movement.

Russian troops moved in when the republic of Chechnya declared its independence from Russia. Both sides sustained heavy casualties in the brutal fighting that ensued.

CHECHNYA is one of the republics of **Russia**, located in the **Caucasus**; its 1 million inhabitants are Muslims. Chechnya declared independence in 1991; its disagreements with Russia were peaceful until December 1994, when Russian troops were sent in. The bombing of the presidential palace in **Grozny** was witnessed on television throughout the world. In July 1995, after a daring attack by Chechens on the Russian city of Budyonnovsk, Chechnya and Russia signed an agreement to solve their dispute peacefully; however, but tensions persist. Chechens are reputedly involved in many **mafia** activities.

CLINTON, BILL (1946–), the forty-second president of the **United States**, promised to turn the attention of his government to domestic American problems. As his term progressed, Clinton began to pay more attention to

U.S. President Bill Clinton played a prominent role in getting talks under way between the representatives of the warring factions in the former Yugoslavia.

foreign affairs; in late 1995, he played a key role in efforts to end the war in **Bosnia and Herzegovina**.

COLD WAR. During World War II, the **U.S.S.R.** was one of the four major Allies who fought against **Germany**. Signs of tensions between the U.S.S.R. and the other three allies—the **United States**, Great Britain, and France—appeared as early as 1945, and soon developed into a full-blown break. During the next four decades, the Cold War was most clearly manifested in regional conflicts, in which the United States and the Soviet Union were always on opposite sides. The enmity between the two superpowers was at its most intense in the early 1950s; later, antagonism alternated with periods of more friendly relations, particularly during the years of **détente** in the 1970s.

By the end of 1990, the Cold War had been officially proclaimed dead. The first test of the new world order was the crisis that developed when Iraq invaded Kuwait in August 1990: it was the first time since World War II that the Soviet Union and the United States were on the same side during an international crisis.

In a sure sign that Cold War tensions had eased, the Soviet Union gradually withdrew its troops from Eastern Europe after its former satellite countries there rejected Communism.

COMECON, or CMEA (Council for Mutual Economic Assistance), was an economic grouping of Communist countries founded in 1949. By the

1980s, it included **Bulgaria**, **Czechoslovakia**, **East Germany**, **Hungary**, **Poland**, **Romania**, and the **U.S.S.R.** in Europe; non-European members were Cuba, Mongolia, and Vietnam. **Albania** was a member from 1949 to 1968. COMECON was set up to promote the "socialist economic organization," but its only important achievement was a flow of cheap oil and raw materials from the Soviet Union to **Eastern Europe**. COMECON disbanded in June 1991.

COMMONWEALTH OF INDEPENDENT STATES (CIS) was first established by the leaders of **Russia**, **Ukraine**, and **Belarus** on December 8, 1991, in Minsk, the capital of Belarus. These leaders announced that they considered the **U.S.S.R.** defunct and that they therefore created a new body which was open to all former Soviet republics. On December 21, 1991, the three original founders of the CIS were joined by the other Soviet republics, with the exception of the **Baltic Republics** and **Georgia**. **Azerbaijan** left the CIS for a year, from October 1992 to September 1993; Georgia joined the organization in December 1993.

Created as a replacement for the old Soviet Union, the CIS lingers on, mainly as a vehicle through which Russia can exert influence over its "near abroad," that is, the former Soviet republics.

COMMUNISM is a word dating from the mid-19th century. The vision of Communism as a classless and economically equitable society was first formulated by Karl Marx in collaboration with Friedrich Engels in the *Communist Manifesto*, published in 1848. The first sentence of the booklet reads, "The specter of Communism is stalking Europe," and it proved to be correct, albeit in a different way than Marx had in mind. The manifesto concludes with a ringing appeal, "Workers of the world, unite!," a phrase that later became one of the magic formulas of **Marxism-Leninism**. In a bitter joke, one banner at Moscow's seventy-second anniversary celebration of the **October Revolution** in 1989 carried a paraphrase, "Workers of the world, forgive us."

CONFERENCE ON SECURITY AND COOPERATION IN EUROPE grew out of the **Helsinki Accords**, signed by 35 countries in 1975. The crowning achievement of this organization was the treaty limiting conventional weapons systems in Europe, concluded in November 1990.

Despite efforts by some post-Communist leaders to make this grouping a chief European forum, the Conference has gradually lost what little influence it ever had. It has an office in Prague, **Czech Republic**, but without any broader institutional framework, it is quite powerless. Renamed Organization for Security and Cooperation in Europe, it tried to stop the fighting in **Nagorny Karabakh** in 1993 and in **Chechnya** in 1995, but with no results.

CRIMEA, a peninsula jutting into the Black Sea, became part of **Russia** in the late 18th century. In 1954, **Nikita Khrushchev** "gave" Crimea to **Ukraine** as an expression of friendship between the peoples of these two republics. It was an empty gesture at that time because everything was decided in Moscow anyway. In 1991, however, when Russia and Ukraine became independent, the status of Crimea began to cause problems. Most inhabitants are ethnic Russians and the port of Sevastopol is home to the rusting Black Sea Fleet, consisting of about 350 ships. In early 1995, Russia and Ukraine decided to divide the fleet between themselves.

Pro-Russian and anti-Ukraine sentiments and rhetoric were particularly strong in 1992 and 1993. In March 1995, the Ukrainian government in Kiev annulled the Crimean constitution and brought the peninsula's parliament under central rule.

CROATIA, one of the six former constituent republics of **Yugoslavia**, is twice as large as Maryland and has about 4.8 million people, more than 11 percent of whom are ethnic Serbs. Croats are Roman Catholics, use the Latin script, and have for centuries considered themselves part of Western Christendom.

Croatia's declaration of independence in June 1991 provoked armed clashes in areas inhabited mostly by Serbs. By the end of the year, about one-third of Croatian territory had been overrun and lost to Serbs, who established a so-called republic of Krajina there. Some 50,000 Croats fled to **Hungary**. After dozens of cease-fires negotiated by the United Nations and the **European Communities** had been broken, the fighting finally subsided and U.N. peacekeeping forces were deployed in the contested areas in early 1992.

President **Franjo Tudjman** is head of the right-of-center, nationalist Croatian Democratic Union (CDU). His popularity and stature rose in 1995 after Croatia, in two quick operations, seized back the territory held by Serbs. Despite a rising **personality cult** around the president, Croatia remains democratic, with a free press and a functioning political opposition. In the October 1995 parliamentary elections, the CDU received 45 percent of the vote.

CZECHOSLOVAKIA was for most of the 20th century a country in the center of Europe; in January 1993, it split into two parts, the **Czech Republic** and **Slovakia**. Rising from the ashes of the Austro-Hungarian Empire at the end of World War I, Czechoslovakia combined the historic lands of Bohemia and Moravia with Slovakia, inhabited by close linguistic cousins of Czechs and Moravians. A strong German minority lived in the border regions. In 1938, Czechoslovakia disintegrated under the onslaught of Nazism.

Communist rule was established in February 1948, and a harsh regime persisted into the early 1960s. A gradual reformist process then culminated in the **Prague Spring** of 1968. After the **Warsaw Pact** invasion in August 1968, a hard-line leadership was installed, and the country plunged into two stuporous decades of "normalization," during which most people retreated into their private worlds. The handful of brave men and women who opposed the repression were harassed and jailed. These **dissidents** became loosely grouped around the **Charter 77** movement.

The country began to stir from its slumber in August 1988, and the Communist regime was toppled the following year, during the "velvet revolution" of November-December 1989. The dissident playwright **Václav Havel** was elected president in late December.

Within a year, the exhilaration triggered by the new freedoms was replaced by the challenges of post-Communist transformation. One problem that soon overshadowed all the others was the friction between Czechs and Slovaks. After the June 1992 elections, in which **Václav Klaus**

In Prague (above), citizens have eagerly embraced the less-restrictive atmosphere that has prevailed since the fall of Communism. The same phenomenon is evident throughout all the former Iron Curtain countries.

and **Vladimír Mečiar** won the respective premierships, Czechoslovakia entered the last six months of its existence. The peaceful "velvet divorce" was finalized on January 1, 1993.

CZECH REPUBLIC is a new country created in 1993 from the western part of **Czechoslovakia**; it is about the size of South Carolina and has a population of 10.3 million. From the 10th century until 1806, the country's two historic regions, Bohemia and Moravia, were an autonomous political entity of the Holy Roman Empire; they later became part of the Austro-Hungarian Empire. In the late 19th century, Bohemia and Moravia were home to 80 percent of the industry of the whole empire, a tradition that fully blossomed during the interwar period, when Czechoslovakia was one of 10 wealthiest countries in the world (relative to its population).

Most Czechs did not want to split Czechoslovakia, but once the split happened, they concentrated on making their new state free and prosperous. By 1995, the country was hailed as the leader of post-Communist rebuilding. The historic capital of Prague, for decades neglected and shabby, is becoming a cosmopolitan metropolis.

In November 1995, the Czech Republic was the first former Communist country to become a member of the OECD (Organization for Economic Cooperation and Development). It is the only country whose two leaders, President **Václav Havel** and Prime Minister **Václav Klaus**, had never been members of the Communist party.

DE-STALINIZATION was initiated by the Soviet leader **Nikita Khrushchev** shortly after his "secret speech" of February 1956, in which he denounced **Stalin**'s reign of terror. De-Stalinization consisted of the dismantling of the vast prison system, or "gulag," later described by **Aleksandr Solzhenitsyn**; a cultural "thaw" that permitted the publishing of unorthodox authors; the elimination of the **personality cult**; and dialogue with the West. Khrushchev's speech was not published in the Soviet Union until early 1989.

DÉTENTE, which means the relaxing of political tensions between countries, started in 1970 when West German chancellor **Willy Brandt** embarked on his policy of conciliation with **East Germany**. The détente culminated in the **Helsinki Accords** of 1975 and ended with the Soviet invasion of Afghanistan in December 1979.

DISSIDENT is a term that came into general use in the 1970s; it designated dissenting individuals or groups in Communist countries. Dissidents were harassed, sometimes put in prison, and later often exiled to the West. The most famous case was the forced exile of **Aleksandr Solzhenitsyn** in 1974. All the dissident movements, with the exception of Polish **Solidarity**, were numerically small, but they represented the seeds of the forthcoming revolutionary upheaval. Some former dissidents then became presidents, prime ministers, and high government officials in the new post-Communist governments.

DNESTR REPUBLIC, or more precisely, Trans-Dniester Republic, is a narrow strip of land along the left bank of the River Dnestr in eastern **Moldova**, where about 40 percent of Moldovan industry is situated. The Slavic inhabitants of this area, fearing the domination of ethnically Romanian Moldovans, declared independence in late 1991. Fighting between the Dnestr National Guard and the Moldovan police erupted in March 1992 and continued for several months, claiming many lives. A peacekeeping force of the **Commonwealth of Independent States (CIS)**, deployed in the region in late summer of 1992, has brought peace and an autonomous status to the area.

DUBČEK, ALEXANDER (1921–92), known in the West as the leader of the **Prague Spring**, was born a few months after his parents had returned from Chicago to their native **Slovakia**, and then spent his youth in the **U.S.S.R.** In early 1968, when he announced his program of "**socialism** with a human face," Dubček became a symbol of hope during a euphoric eight-month liberalization period. After August 1968, he was expelled from the party and made a "nonperson."

During the "velvet revolution" in November 1989, Dubček came to Prague, and then became the chairman of the Federal Assembly. He died from injuries incurred in a car accident.

EASTERN EUROPE. This term designated the European Communist countries. Since Europe extends from the Atlantic Ocean in the west to the Ural Mountains in the east, "Eastern Europe" is a misnomer: **Poland**, the **Czech Republic**, **Slovakia**, **Hungary**, and the former **East Germany** lie in the center of Europe. People in these countries have always felt that they belong to Western European civilization.

The southern four countries belonging to the political group of "Eastern Europe"—**Romania**, **Bulgaria**, **Yugoslavia**, and **Albania**—are more properly called the Balkan countries, and have historically composed that part of southeastern Europe influenced by Orthodox Christianity and the Ottoman Empire.

EAST GERMANY was a Communist state known formally as the German Democratic Republic; it existed from October 7, 1949, until October 2, 1990—40 years and 360 days. Almost the same size as Tennessee, the country had 16 million people.

In 1945, the defeated Nazi **Germany** was divided into four occupation zones. As the World War II Allies—the **United States**, Britain, France, and the **U.S.S.R.**—drifted apart in the first years of the **Cold War**, the three western zones were combined into the Federal Republic of

Germany in 1949. Shortly after that, the Soviet zone became the German Democratic Republic.

The first half of East German existence was characterized by a stringent hostility toward West Germany, culminating in the erection of the **Berlin Wall** in 1961. The second half, when the party was headed by **Erich Honecker**, was ushered in by **Willy Brandt**'s *Ostpolitik,* a policy of conciliation between the two German states.

Economically better off than people in other Communist states, East Germans had two major grievances: they were constantly comparing themselves to their wealthier West German kin, and they bitterly resented the prohibition of foreign travel. When the **Iron Curtain** along the Austro-Hungarian border cracked in the summer of 1989, thousands of East German tourists vacationing in **Hungary** started pouring through. Their dramatic exodus was followed by television viewers throughout the world. In September, demonstrations started in East German cities; and on October 18, Erich Honecker resigned. His successor, Egon Krenz, had his moment of glory on November 9, when he ordered the **Berlin Wall** opened. After several months of political turmoil, the first free East German elections took place in March 1990.

Meanwhile, West German chancellor **Helmut Kohl** was pursuing his plan for reunification. In March 1990, the "two plus four" (two Germanies plus the United States, Britain, France, and the U.S.S.R.) reunification talks opened in Bonn, and on September 12, 1990, the *Final Settlement with Respect to Germany* was signed. It was the formal end of World War II.

This treaty led to German reunification, which took effect at midnight on October 2, 1990. East Germany was incorporated—as five newly constituted states—into the Federal Republic of Germany.

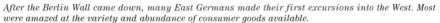

After the Berlin Wall came down, many East Germans made their first excursions into the West. Most were amazed at the variety and abundance of consumer goods available.

ESTONIA, the northernmost of the three **Baltic Republics**, is about twice the size of Massachusetts. Out of its 1.5 million inhabitants, only 62 percent speak Estonian—an Ugro-Finnic language related to Finnish and Hungarian. The most Western of all former Soviet republics, Estonia has a distinct Scandinavian look.

A law adopted in 1992 granted automatic citizenship only to those inhabitants of Estonia, or their descendants, who had lived there before the 1940 annexation by the **U.S.S.R.** Most of the ethnic Russians who had moved to Estonia during the Soviet period were thus excluded from citizenship. This issue contributed to tensions with **Russia** over the withdrawal of troops, but the last Russian soldiers finally left Estonia on August 31, 1994.

Estonia has gone farthest in post-Communist economic transformations, but economic hardships experienced by a large part of the population led to the victory of former Communists in parliamentary elections in March 1995.

ETHNIC CLEANSING was the term used by Serbians for the forced evacuations of non-Serb inhabitants from the captured areas in **Bosnia and Herzegovina** and for the creation of "ethnically pure" regions. The policy was unanimously condemned by a U.N. Security Council resolution in August 1992. By 1995, approximately 2 million people in the former **Yugoslavia** had become victims of ethnic cleansing.

EUROPEAN COMMUNITIES was a collective name given to three different yet related organizations: the European Economic Community (EEC), also known as the Common Market, which was established in 1958 for the purpose of integrating the economies of Western Europe; the European Coal and Steel Community (ESCS), which was established in 1952 as a precursor of the EEC; and the European Atomic Energy Community (EURATOM), which was established in January 1958, at the same time as the Common Market. The central institutions of these three communities were merged in July 1967; they include the Council of Ministers, the Commission, the European Parliament, the Court of Justice, and the European Council. The 12 full members of the EC were: Belgium, Denmark, France, **Germany**, Greece, Ireland, Italy, Luxembourg, Netherlands, Portugal, Spain, and United Kingdom. The European Communities became the **European Union** on the basis of the **Maastricht Treaty**, signed in December 1991.

EUROPEAN UNION (EU), which became effective on November 1, 1993, is the successor to the **European Communities**. Four new members—Norway, Austria, Sweden, and Finland—were admitted in 1993 and 1994, pending approval in national referendums. The Norwegian voters rejected joining the EU, but voters in the other three countries voted yes. Most European former Communist countries are eager to join the union and have been discussing the terms and dates with **Brussels** and with EU member governments.

GEORGIA, a former Soviet republic, is somewhat larger than West Virginia; its 5.5 million inhabitants are proud heirs to a more than 2,000-year-old history. The majority of Georgians are Christians, but there are significant Muslim minorities. The most famous (or rather, infamous) Georgian was Josif Vissarionovich Dzhugashvili, who early in his career adopted the surname **Stalin**.

In April 1989, Soviet troops attacked a nationalist demonstration in the Georgian capital, Tbilisi, and clubbed 20 people to death. This event led to an increased agitation for independence from the **U.S.S.R.**. When Georgia finally did gain independence in late 1991, it was already embroiled in ethnic wars in **Abkhazia** and South **Ossetia** that rapidly sapped its energy. By 1994, the fighting had brought the country to the brink of almost total collapse.

The first popularly elected leader of a Soviet republic was the former **dissident** Zviad Gamsakhurdia, who became Georgia's president in May 1991. He campaigned on a platform of messianic nationalism, but soon alienated large segments of the population with his dictatorial behavior. Fighting between his supporters and opponents led to Gamsakhurdia's ouster in January 1992. After several months, **Eduard Shevardnadze** returned to Georgia and became chairman of the state council. Trying without success to bring the country to peace, Shevardnadze finally called in the Russians and allowed them to set up military bases in Georgia, in return for their help in stopping the regional wars.

GERMANY is the wealthiest country in Europe and, after **Russia**, the most populous, with 81.2 million inhabitants. Germans, like the French, trace

In 1989, East and West Germans gathered triumphantly on the crumbling Berlin Wall. The euphoria was short-lived, however, as the country began to face the problems associated with reunification.

the beginnings of their political history to Charlemagne. In contrast to the French, however, Germans were first united into one state only in the late 19th century. During the Middle Ages and early modern period, present-day Germany consisted of a multitude of smaller principalities that had been part of the Holy Roman Empire (together with most of Italy, Austria, Bohemia, and other regions). The "Iron Chancellor" Otto Bismarck, a Prussian statesman, engineered German unification in 1871. The new state, eager to take its place alongside the major European powers, began to pursue an aggressive expansionist policy, which eventually led to the outbreak of World War I in 1914. Crushed in a humiliating defeat, Germany tried to rebound after the war, but was hampered by the burden of reparations, combined with worldwide economic depression—conditions that ultimately led to the rise of Adolf Hitler.

After World War II, Germany was divided into Communist **East Germany** and the democratic Federal Republic of Germany (West Germany). The latter profited from generous U.S. help through the **Marshall Plan**; the amazing West German recuperation after World War II was often called an economic miracle. Equally important was the development of grassroots democracy.

The second German unification, in 1991—led by Chancellor **Helmut Kohl**—created a powerful new country in the heart of Europe, albeit at an almost overwhelming cost. The economy of the former East Germany virtually collapsed, and tensions between East Germans and their Western relatives persist. The Easterners (Ossis) complain about the condescending attitudes of Westerners (Wessis), who in turn criticize the laziness of their new fellow citizens. Despite unmistakable economic improvement, in mid-1995 two-thirds of East Germans thought that a "well-managed" socialism is preferable to a free-market economy.

GLASNOST, a term introduced by **Mikhail Gorbachev**, became an international household word in the late 1980s. Meaning "openness," it referred to a free public debate about social, political, and economic matters, and about the past. *Glasnost* was a traumatic experience for many Soviet citizens, especially the older ones, because it undermined almost all certainties and rules.

Conceived as one of the means to achieve *perestroika*, a transformation of the Soviet system, *glasnost* was ultimately one of the agents leading to the collapse of the **U.S.S.R.**

GÖNCZ, ÁRPÁD, (1922–), president of **Hungary** since 1990. He is a writer and former **dissident**, who had been sentenced to death for his part in the Hungarian uprising of 1956. He has no actual power, but is very popular and, because of his grandfatherly touch, is often referred to as "Papa Göncz."

GORBACHEV, MIKHAIL (1931–), the last Soviet leader, was general secretary of the Communist Party of the **U.S.S.R.** from March 1985 to August 1991, president of the U.S.S.R. from March 1990 to December 1991, and a Nobel Peace Prize winner in 1990. Forceful and somewhat pompous, Gorbachev tried to reform the Soviet system, but failed. It was his rival and opponent, **Boris Yeltsin**, who stepped through the opened door and into the new era.

Praised and criticized by many, Gorbachev had two strong points: he believed in freedom of speech and he refused to use force to achieve political goals. In retirement since late 1991, he heads the Gorbachev Foundation, a think tank with some 100 staffers; he continues to cherish political ambitions.

GROZNY, the capital of the Russian republic of **Chechnya**, was mercilessly bombed by Russian troops in early 1995 and was largely destroyed.

HAVEL, VÁCLAV (1937–), playwright, writer, **dissident**, the last president of **Czechoslovakia**

Mikhail Gorbachev, with his policies of glasnost and perestroika, set in motion the events that led to the fall of Communism in Eastern Europe and, ultimately, in the Soviet Union.

(December 1989 to July 1992), and the first president of the **Czech Republic** (since January 1993). Born into a wealthy family, Havel was not admitted to a secondary school because he was branded a "class enemy."

One of the founders of the **Charter 77** movement, he spent more than four years in prison. In November 1989, Havel led the Czechoslovak "velvet revolution." He does not have much actual power, but he remains one of the most popular politicians in the post-Communist world, with a steady approval rating of about 70 percent.

Václav Havel, a prominent Czech dissident, was the last president of Czechoslovakia and the first president of the Czech Republic.

HELSINKI ACCORDS were the first document of the **Conference on Security and Cooperation in Europe**, signed in 1975 in Helsinki, the capital of Finland. The document guaranteed the inviolability of European borders and included pledges to respect human rights. The Helsinki Accords were at the time denounced by some as a sellout to the **U.S.S.R.**, but they ultimately played a positive role in the unraveling of Communist regimes. **Dissident** "Helsinki groups" emerged in many countries and demanded from their governments respect for human rights.

HONECKER, ERICH (1912–94), was the leader of East German Communist Party from 1971, and head of **East Germany** as Chairman of the State Council until he was deposed in October 1989. He presided over a rapprochement between the two Germanies.

In March 1991, after the German reunification, Honecker fled to Moscow, finding asylum in the Chilean embassy there. In July 1992, he was flown back to Berlin to face charges of misappropriation of state funds and manslaughter, the latter in connection with the "**shoot-to-kill**" policy of East German government. The next year, however, he was freed because of advanced cancer; he eventually returned to Chile, where he died in May 1994.

HUNGARY is a flat, landlocked country in the center of Europe, somewhat smaller than Indiana. Its 10.3 million inhabitants are descendants of warrior-nomad Magyar tribes that came to central Europe from Asia in the 9th century. They settled down, accepted Christianity, and later formed an important medieval kingdom.

In the 19th century, Hungary gained an internal autonomy within the Austro-Hungarian Empire. When the empire collapsed at the end of World War I, Hungary lost about two-thirds of its territory to **Romania** and the newly formed countries of **Czechoslovakia** and **Yugoslavia**. Large Hungarian minorities continue to live in **Slovakia**, Romanian Transylvania, and **Croatia**.

In 1941, Hungary joined World War II on the side of **Germany**. After the war, the Hungarian Communists took power with the help of Soviet occupying forces. A simmering anti-Communist and anti-Soviet resentment gradually festered into open revolt in November 1956. The uprising was brutally suppressed; the estimates of people killed range from 6,500 to 32,000. About 250 participants, including the hero of the uprising, Imre Nagy, were later executed.

The era of **János Kádár**, who was installed as premier by the Soviets, saw many political and economic reforms. The Hungarian system, branded by **Nikita Khrushchev** as "goulash **Communism**," gradually evolved into one of the most liberal Communist regimes.

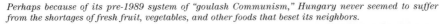

Perhaps because of its pre-1989 system of "goulash Communism," Hungary never seemed to suffer from the shortages of fresh fruit, vegetables, and other foods that beset its neighbors.

In the late 1980s, the authority of the Communist Party began to erode. In October 1989, the party was dissolved and reconstituted as the Hungarian Socialist Party. At the same time, opposition forces crystallized into several groupings. Meanwhile, by opening its borders with Austria in the summer of 1989, Hungary ushered in the final brief chapter for European Communist regimes. They fell one after another, like dominos.

Hungarians might have felt a little cheated because their transition to the post-Communist era was quiet and undramatic. The first free elections since 1946 took place in March and April 1990, and the rightist Hungarian Democratic Forum emerged as the winner. The subsequent political calm, punctured occasionally by government scandals and extremist pronouncements, was not even greatly upset by the parliamentary victory of former Communists in May 1994.

Hungarians were the first ones to start economic transformation, long before their central European neighbors, but by 1995 they were lagging behind **Poland** and the **Czech Republic**, with a large foreign debt and uncompleted **privatization** of state enterprises and land.

ILIESCU, ION (1930–), the suave leader of the Romanian National Salvation Front (NSF), was elected president of **Romania** in May 1990, with 85 percent of the vote. Iliescu had studied in Moscow, and then held senior posts in regional administration, but in the 1980s was pushed aside by **Nicolae Ceauşescu**. Although opposition leaders have repeatedly charged that Iliescu's commitment to democracy and market economy was insincere, Iliescu was nonetheless elected by a 60 percent majority to his second presidential term in 1992.

IRON CURTAIN. In a speech in Missouri on March 15, 1946, Sir Winston Churchill said that "an Iron Curtain has descended over the continent." Thus was coined the term that for decades would describe the heavily fortified and virtually impenetrable border between the West and the Communist countries. The Iron Curtain stretched from the Baltic Sea in the north to Trieste in the south. An extension was added in 1961 with the erection of the **Berlin Wall**.

IZETBEGOVIĆ, ALIJA (1925–), president of independent **Bosnia and Herzegovina** since March 1992, is a former Communist and a Muslim scholar. He has repeatedly pledged a commitment to a democratic and multiethnic Bosnia and Herzegovina, even though some observers criticize him for a certain nationalist intolerance. His steadfast efforts to solve the crisis in his country finally culminated in the peace agreement reached in Dayton, Ohio, in November 1995.

In his role as president of Bosnia and Herzegovina, Alija Izetbegović sought ways to help end the onslaught of Bosnian Serbs.

JARUZELSKI, WOJCIECH (1923–), general of the Polish army, became prime minister of **Poland** in March 1981, during the heyday of **Solidarity**. Under intense Soviet pressure to suppress the "antisocialist" forces in the country, he declared martial law in December 1981 and had the Solidarity leaders, including **Lech Wałęsa**, arrested. In July 1989, Jaruzelski was elected president of Poland, a position he retained until November 1990. He was succeeded by Wałęsa.

As Polish prime minister, Wojciech Jaruzelski (center, at a wreath-laying ceremony) led the 1981 crackdown on Solidarity, in part to avoid possible Soviet military intervention.

JOHN PAUL II (1920–). Karol Wojtyła, archbishop of Cracow, **Poland**, was elevated to the papacy in 1978, the first Slav ever to occupy the highest post in the Roman Catholic Church. He greatly contributed to the determination of his Polish compatriots to challenge **Communism**. In December 1989, John Paul II had a 75-minute private audience with **Mikhail Gorbachev**, the first meeting ever between a pope and a Soviet leader. In the early 1990s, the pope traveled to many post-Communist countries.

KÁDÁR, JÁNOS (1912–89), was the Hungarian Communist leader between 1956 and 1988. Coming to power during the 1956 uprising, with Soviet backing, Kádár became known as the "butcher of Budapest." In 1961, however, he initiated a period of national conciliation by proclaiming; "Whoever is not against us is with us." A sweeping amnesty in 1962 and subsequent economic liberalizations made **Hungary** the most liberal country in **Eastern Europe**.

Late in life, Kádár gradually became resistant to economic reforms. Finally, in 1988, he was "kicked upstairs" to the essentially ceremonial post of party president. He died a few months before Hungary discarded Communism.

KARADŽIĆ, RADOVAN (1944–), a psychiatrist by profession, became president and supreme commander of the Bosnian Serbs in 1992. He was indicted by the international court at The Hague as one of the chief war criminals of the war in **Bosnia and Herzegovina**.

KARIMOV, ISLAM (1938–), the president of **Uzbekistan** since 1990, is a former Communist who apparently still believes that a centralized economic system will lead to prosperity. Karimov courts Westerners in order to attract foreign investment, but also disregards human rights and maintains tight control over the population. He claims that western democracy cannot be implemented in Central Asia at this point.

Islam Karimov (above, at right), the president of Uzbekistan, is perhaps most noted for his resistance to reforms and the tight control he exercises over the population.

KAZAKHSTAN, a Central Asian republic four times the size of Texas, has a population of about 17 million. Part of the **U.S.S.R.** until 1991, Kazakhstan was one of the four Soviet republics with nuclear weapons located within its borders. In 1993, the government approved the Nuclear Non-Proliferation Treaty; the **United States** then agreed to finance denuclearization. The space center at Baikonur continues to be used by the **Commonwealth of Independent States (CIS)**.

Historically a land of nomadic horsemen, Kazakhstan was transformed during the Soviet period into a country with huge cotton plantations and heavily polluted industrial urban centers. It is rich in minerals,

Kazakhstan's leader Nursultan Nazarbayev has emerged as one of the most powerful leaders in the former Soviet republics. His lobbying efforts have brought much foreign investment to his country.

with oil fields rivaling Alaska's Prudhoe Bay, and about half of the world's uranium reserves. In May 1992, the republic's leader, **Nursultan Nazarbayev**, signed a multibillion-dollar investment deal with Chevron, a U.S. oil company, for the development of the Tenghiz oil fields near the Caspian Sea. The influence of **Russia** continues to be very strong.

KHRUSHCHEV, NIKITA (1894–1971), a Soviet leader who began his political career under **Stalin**. After the dictator's death, Khrushchev shocked the Soviet Communist Party—and the rest of the world—with his "secret speech" of February 1956, in which he denounced Stalin's crimes and initiated the period of so-called "**de-Stalinization**." A timid precursor of **Mikhail Gorbachev**, Khrushchev was forced out of office in 1964. In the last years of his life, he secretly dictated his memoirs, which were published in the West.

KLAUS, VÁCLAV (1941–), prime minister of the **Czech Republic** from January 1993, is leader of the center-right Civic Democratic Party. Klaus emerged as an articulate, urbane politician in 1990 and became known as the architect of the coupon **privatization** system. He is well known in Western capitals and admired for his intellectual brilliance, but many Czechs dislike his overbearing personality. His popularity is high nevertheless, particularly among the educated and the entrepreneurs.

German chancellor Helmut Kohl presided over the fall of the Berlin Wall and the reunification of East and West Germany. In 1990, he became the first leader of the reunited Germany.

KOHL, HELMUT (1930–), the head of the German Christian Democratic Party, German chancellor, and the chief engineer of German reunification. One of Kohl's greatest moments was in July 1990, when he emerged from a meeting with **Mikhail Gorbachev** and announced that the **U.S.S.R.** had agreed to the participation of the united Germany in **NATO**. Kohl is the main advocate of European integration.

KOSOVO is a small region in southern **Serbia**. Most of its inhabitants are ethnic Albanians who have fought for greater autonomy. Their conflict with local Serbs was particularly bloody in the late 1980s, resulting in dozens of casualties. By mid-1990, the violence had subsided somewhat, although tensions persist.

In one of the many conflicts under way in what was formerly Yugoslavia, the ethnic Albanian majority who live in the Kosovo region of Serbia are agitating for greater autonomy.

KYRGYZSTAN, a Central Asian country about the size of South Dakota, has 4.5 million people. Known as Kirghizia in the Soviet period, the republic lies in the remote ranges of the Tien Shan mountains.

Although president Askar Akayev dismissed the parliament in September 1994, he does—in contrast to the leaders in neighboring countries—tolerate political opposition. He wants to privatize the land and restore Russian as a national language in order to stem the exodus of the skilled Russians who used to run the economy.

LATVIA, one of the three **Baltic Republics**, is almost the same size as West Virginia; of its 2.5 million inhabitants, only 53 percent are ethnic Latvians. In May 1990, the Latvian Supreme Soviet declared the republic's independence, but it took more than a year before the country definitively shook off Soviet rule.

A law passed in 1992 granted citizenship to ethnic Latvians only; thus, almost half of the population, mostly ethnic Russians and Ukrainians, became noncitizens: they cannot vote, cannot own land, and are prohibited from working in many government jobs. This law delayed the final withdrawal of Russian troops until August 1994.

By 1995, the economic situation had stabilized to a certain extent. In parliamentary elections held in the summer of 1995, a strange mixture of political leaders emerged, consisting of emigrés, fascists, and former Communist officials.

LITHUANIA, the southernmost of the three **Baltic Republics**, is slightly larger than West Virginia and has a population of 3.7 million. Medieval Lithuania embraced a much larger territory than the present republic, and often was at loggerheads with **Russia**.

Lithuania was the first Soviet republic to initiate secession from the **U.S.S.R.** The independence drive was led by the Lithuania Restructuring

Lithuania was the first Soviet republic to initiate secession from the Soviet Union. Independence finally came in September 1991 following the failed coup in Moscow.

Movement, known as *Sajudis*, and its leader, musicologist Vytautas Landsbergis. In March 1990, Lithuania declared its independence and elected Landsbergis president, but true independence came only in September 1991.

One year later, disgruntled with economic hardships and disillusioned by political infighting within the *Sajudis* movement, 45 percent of the Lithuanian electorate voted in parliamentary elections for reform-minded former Communists led by Algirdas Brazauskas.

MAASTRICHT TREATY, signed by the 12 members of the **European Communities** in December 1991, in Maastricht, the Netherlands, provided for closer European integration and the gradual lifting of all trade barriers, and called for a common European currency by the end of the century. Once the treaty had been ratified by the electorate in all 12 countries (in October 1993), the European Communities became known as the **European Union**.

Vytautas Landsbergis (right) led the Lithuanian drive for independence. In late 1992, his Sajudis party was defeated in the polls by former Communists.

MACEDONIA is the name of a former constituent republic of **Yugoslavia** that declared independence in 1991. Macedonia is also the name of a historic region in the Balkan Peninsula that richly plays into Greek heritage. This twofold usage of the word has caused serious problems: Greece has blocked the republic's international recognition, claiming that the name "Macedonia" and its new state symbols actually belong to Greek history. In April 1993, the new state was admitted to the United Nations under the provisional name of The Former Yugoslav Republic of Macedonia. The **United States** recognized Macedonia as a state in February 1994.

Macedonia is slightly larger than Vermont. Its 2.1 million people include a large Albanian minority and a smaller Serbian minority. The country has been an oasis of peace, although the unsuccessful attempt to assassinate its president, Kiro Gligorov, in October 1995 raised fears that nationalist, anti-Greek passions might emerge. The president is the leading advocate of a compromise with Greece.

MAFIA. With the collapse of the **U.S.S.R.**, there has been a great rise in international organized crime, in which the Russian mafia plays a significant role. According to knowledgeable police officials, the Italian Cosa Nostra pales in comparison with this new international network. Connections with Israel, which has become a haven for "dirty money," and with former Soviet officials add extra clout. Reputedly, nine Russian mafia "families" have divided the world among themselves. Their specialties are drugs and nuclear material.

MARSHALL PLAN, a "European Recovery Program," was extended by the **United States** to European nations to help them overcome the ravages of World War II. The $11 billion dispensed from 1947 to 1951 was instrumental in rebuilding West **Germany**, which had been virtually destroyed, as well as other nations. The aid was also offered in 1947 to some central European nations, such as **Czechoslovakia**, **Poland**, and **Hungary**, an offer vetoed by Moscow.

MARXISM-LENINISM was the term for the ideological package that several generations of children and adults in the Communist countries were taught in schools and obligatory seminars. The main pillars of this ideology were:

- All human history until the **October Revolution** was characterized by class struggle between the rich and the poor.
- The **U.S.S.R.** is the protector of all the oppressed peoples in the world.
- The Communist Party is the most progressive force in the society.
- The imperialists, led by the **United States**, exploit workers and peasants and support rightist dictators all around the world.
- The socialist economy is the only scientific system that has eliminated exploitation and brought equality to all citizens.

MEČIAR, VLADIMÍR (1943–), is the prime minister of **Slovakia**. A former Communist, Mečiar began to press for greater Slovak autonomy during 1991, gradually alienating a large segment of **Czechoslovakia**'s Czech population with his brash style and populist demagogy. He was one of the main architects of the splitting of Czechoslovakia into two countries. In early 1994, Mečiar lost his premiership, but he regained it in September 1994 elections. He remains the most popular Slovak politician, but his campaign to depose president Michal Kováč earned him official criticism from the **European Union** for his disregard of basic democratic practices.

MILOŠEVIĆ, SLOBODAN (1941–), president of **Serbia** since 1987, has been vilified for fanning the nationalist conflict in **Yugoslavia**; he has been dubbed the "butcher of the Balkans." His plan to create a "Greater Serbia" has incited ethnic Serbs in **Croatia** and **Bosnia and Herzegovina** to take up arms against Croats and Muslims. In late 1992, he was reelected president of Serbia by 56 percent of the voters.

Serbian president Slobodan Milošević, the notorious "butcher of the Balkans," is blamed for inciting much of the conflict in the former Yugoslavia.

Gradually, Milošević became a key player in peace negotiations, probably because he grew tired of a war that was impoverishing his country; from 1994 onward, he pressured the Bosnian Serbs to come to an agreement with the Muslim government. With **Franjo Tudjman** of Croatia and **Alija Izetbegović** of Bosnia and Herzegovina, he signed the November 1995 peace agreement in Dayton, Ohio.

MOLDOVA, the second smallest of the former Soviet republics, is about the size of Massachusetts and Connecticut combined. Historically part of **Romania**, Moldova was annexed to the **U.S.S.R.** in June 1940.

Ethnic Romanians, or Moldovans, represent 66 percent of the country's 4.4 million inhabitants; the rest, mostly living in the eastern part of the country, are predominantly ethnic Russians and Ukrainians. The Moldavian language, virtually identical with Romanian, was made the state language in August 1989, a move which provoked opposition from the Slav minorities. In 1991, the Slavs formed a secessionist "Trans-Dniester Republic" on the left bank of the Dnestr. In the early part of 1992, hundreds of people were killed in clashes between the separatists and the Moldovan security forces.

In just a few short years, Mircea Snegur, the president of Moldova since December 1991, has guided his republic through a massive economic transformation.

That year, the economy suffered not only from the fighting, but also from floods and a drought; things turned around in 1993. A voucher-type **privatization** took place in 1994 and the first stock exchange opened in 1995. Observers began to praise the country's transformation as a "small wonder."

The Moldovan and Romanian governments cautiously discussed the possible uniting of both countries, but in March 1994, Moldovans rejected reunification in a plebiscite. **Mircea Snegur**, the country's president since 1990, uses the phrase "two Romanias," to stress both the kinship and Moldovan independence.

NAGORNY KARABAKH is a small region within **Azerbaijan**; three-quarters of its population are Armenian. The conflict concerning control over this enclave began in 1988 and soon escalated into a full-scale war. A temporary cease-fire was achieved in May 1994, but as of late 1995, the situation remained tense.

NATO (North Atlantic Treaty Organization) was created in 1949 by a treaty between the **United States**, Canada, and 10 West European nations who joined against a common enemy, the Communist **U.S.S.R.** and **Eastern Europe**. Several other nations, including **West Germany**, joined later. It is the world's strongest military organization.

Since the enemy has now undergone a profound transformation, NATO has had to redefine its mission. Central European countries would like to join NATO, but **Russia** is against the enlargement of what it considers to be a threatening organization. Under the **Partnership for Peace** program, NATO has been conducting joint military exercises in some of the former Communist countries. NATO's largest military operation began in 1995 in **Bosnia and Herzegovina**.

NAZARBAYEV, NURSULTAN (1940–), a former Communist and, since 1991, the president of **Kazakhstan**. He is a pragmatic leader, widely popular and respected despite his authoritarian practices. In March 1995, he dismissed parliament because it was blocking his efforts to start land **privatization**. Stressing that the Western political model is not immediately applicable to his country, he says that "democracy is only just knocking at our door."

OCTOBER REVOLUTION, which actually took place on November 7, 1917 (according to the old Russian calendar), in Petrograd (later Leningrad and, since 1991, St. Petersburg), was one of the crucial moments of the 20th century. This event marked the beginning of the Soviet era and of modern **Communism**; until the late 1980s, its anniversary was dutifully hailed in all the Communist capitals. As a sad summation of the "historical significance" of this event, a banner reading "Seventy-Two Years of Going Nowhere" was carried during the 72nd-anniversary celebrations in Moscow. The anniversary is still remembered in some post-Communist countries, mostly by retirees.

OSSETIA is a region in the **Caucasus** consisting of North Ossetia, within **Russia**, and South Ossetia, within **Georgia**. The South Ossetian nationalists wanted to unite their region with North Ossetia and, to accomplish this goal, took to arms in 1989. By 1992, about 1,400 people had been killed. A cease-fire took effect in July 1992.

PARTNERSHIP FOR PEACE is the name of a program of gradual rapprochement that **NATO** offered to the former Communist countries in October 1993. In June 1994, even **Russia** joined the program. The partnership includes joint military exercises and training, consultations, and coordination of peacekeeping efforts.

PERESTROIKA, a Russian word meaning "restructuring" or "reconstruction," entered the international lexicon in 1986, when **Mikhail Gorbachev** set it and *glasnost*, meaning "openness" about present and past problems, as goals. After five years, *perestroika* brought only disarray, shortages, collapse of authority, and ethnic conflict. The expiration of the **U.S.S.R.** in 1991 showed that efforts to transform the Soviet system were futile.

PERSONALITY CULT was a distinctive feature of Communist societies. The first and probably the greatest personality cult enveloped **Stalin**, who was elevated to a godlike position and was praised as the wisest of men, the most beloved leader, the greatest war hero, the most brilliant scientist. Streets and cities were named after Stalin, and monuments to him dotted the Communist world. The most pronounced personality cults in **Eastern Europe** surrounded **Ceauşescu** of **Romania**, **Tito** of **Yugoslavia**, and Enver Hoxha of **Albania**.

POLAND, a flat, New Mexico-sized country in central Europe, has a population of 38.6 million. Poland's history began 1,000 years ago; during the Middle Ages, it emerged as an important Central European kingdom. In the late 18th century, the so-called "three partitions" erased Poland from the map, its territory being divided between **Russia**, Prussia, and Austria. The Polish nation nonetheless survived, and it regained independence in 1918.

In November 1995, Alexander Kwaśniewski defeated the incumbent, Lech Wałęsa, in Poland's presidential elections.

The attack on Poland by Nazi **Germany** in September 1939 was the first act of World War II. As the German armies advanced from the west, Soviet armies entered Poland from the east. Numerous concentration camps were set up on Polish soil, the most infamous of them the extermination camp at Auschwitz.

After the war, Poland was "shifted" westward: its eastern part was retained by the **U.S.S.R.** and, in compensation, the country gained a large territory in the west, which before World War II had belonged to Germany. Communists took over in 1948, and, in the first period, closely followed the Soviet model. In 1956, Polish nationalist and traditionally anti-Russian sentiment, combined with economic grievances, ultimately fueled the eruption of workers' riots in the city of Poznan. The riots brought down the Politburo and elevated Władysław Gomułka to the leadership of the party. He introduced a series of liberal reforms, abolished the farm-collectivization program, and improved relations with the church.

New workers' riots in Gdansk in December 1970 were brutally suppressed, with at least 44 persons killed. Gomułka was replaced by Edward Gierek, who quickly became one of the main proponents of **détente** with the West. Continuing economic hardships, however, precipitated a new wave of protests in 1976.

Two years later, the Polish nation suddenly had a reason to rejoice when the archbishop of Cracow became **Pope John Paul II**. This event played a crucial, albeit indirect, role in the demise of Communism in **Eastern Europe** by giving Poles the courage to challenge their rulers. And so, in August 1980, the famous trade union **Solidarity** was born, and **Lech Wałęsa** became the supreme Polish hero. This also marked the beginning of the decade of **Wojciech Jaruzelski**.

During the 15 months of Solidarity ascendancy, it almost seemed that Communist rule was coming to an end in Poland. In December 1981,

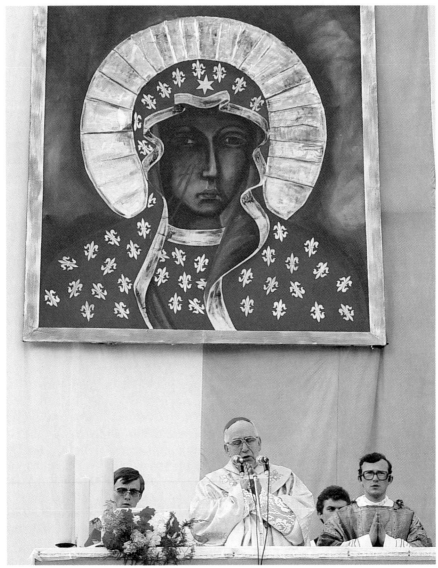

Despite persecution, the Roman Catholic Church retained the devotion of the Polish people throughout the Communist era. The church's influence has waned somewhat in post-Communist Poland.

however, Jaruzelski declared martial law, banned Solidarity, and abolished all the newly gained freedoms.

In 1985, the Soviet Union, now in its final years, gradually loosened its grip over its satellite countries, providing greater room for anti-Communist action. Solidarity regained its legal status in early 1989 and, in the partially free elections of June 1989, it won a resounding victory. In August, Poland had its first non-Communist prime minister since 1948: Tadeusz Mazowiecki, a Catholic intellectual and close friend of Wałęsa. His government set the country on a transition toward a market economy.

A split within Solidarity took place in the summer of 1990, culminating in a presidential contest between Wałęsa and Mazowiecki. The former won the presidency by a landslide in December 1990.

In the first fully free parliamentary elections in October 1991, a center-right coalition came to power, but political paralysis debilitated the country throughout 1992. A multitude of political parties, five prime ministers between October 1991 and the fall of 1992, high unemployment, high inflation, and thousands of farms on the verge of bankruptcy were among the major problems facing Poland. President Wałęsa repeatedly asked the parliament for greater powers to break the political deadlock, but was always rejected.

The former Communists and the other leftist parties that won in the parliamentary elections of September 1993 continued with economic reform. By 1995, Poland was well on its way toward prosperity, with the highest economic growth of all the post-Communist countries. Meanwhile, however, frictions between the parliament and Wałęsa caused several government crises and eventually contributed to the defeat of the former Solidarity hero in his second presidential election, held in November 1995, to a post-Communist candidate, Alexander Kwaśniewski.

PRAGUE SPRING was, in **Czechoslovakia**, the period from early January to August 20, 1968, when, under the leadership of reformist Communist intelligentsia, and with somewhat reluctant support from the Politburo led by **Alexander Dubček**, the regime underwent a series of democratic reforms. The **U.S.S.R.**, headed by **Leonid Brezhnev**, considered these changes too dangerous, and crushed the movement with the help of 500,000 **Warsaw Pact** troops. Asked in 1987 about the difference between the Prague spring and *glasnost* and *perestroika*, a Soviet Foreign Ministry spokesman replied, "nineteen years."

PRICE LIBERALIZATION has been one of the basic components of the economic transformation of former Communist countries. In a command economy, prices were fixed by the government and often remained the same for decades, thanks to large governmental subsidies. In many places, the lifting of price controls led to protests against sudden price increases. Some commodities still remain subsidized, even in countries that have gone the farthest toward market economy: in the **Czech Republic**, for instance, consumers pay artificially low rates for electricity and gas.

PRIVATIZATION of state enterprises in the former Communist countries has been one of the most difficult tasks of the transition to a free-market economy. Among the various schemes tried in several countries so far, the "coupon system" introduced by **Václav Klaus** in **Czechoslovakia** seems to work best. It consists of transforming state enterprises into shareholding companies, with individual shares being distributed among the population. Other ways to privatize include selling companies to private and foreign investors, or distributing shares among employees of each enterprise. Privatization of land in **Eastern Europe** is easier: in most cases, it is returned to its original owners or their descendants. In the former Soviet Union, however, land privatization after seven decades of Communist rule is only in its earliest stages.

By the end of 1994, privatization had been most successful in the **Czech Republic**, where about 65 percent of the national wealth had been transferred into private hands. **Hungary**, **Poland**, and **Slovakia** trailed behind with 55 percent. What is most surprising, however, is that an 18-month program led by a young reformer, Anatoly Chubais, privatized half

Slowly but surely, private enterprise is making its mark in the former Soviet Union. Several U.S. restaurant chains have opened franchises in Moscow and other Russian cities.

of the state economy of **Russia**. Critics point to widespread corruption during this process, but given the political turmoil and the legacy of the Soviet system, the negative aspects were probably inevitable.

REAGAN, RONALD (1911–), the fortieth president of the **United States** (1981-89), was elected less than a year after the Soviet invasion of Afghanistan and, in his first term, called the **U.S.S.R.** "an evil empire." He accelerated the arms race, thus putting additional pressure on the Soviet Union and contributing to the deepening crisis and final demise of the Soviet system.

REFUGEES. One of the most serious problems since the end of the **Cold War** has been the massive displacement of people in many parts of the former Communist bloc. Refugees fled from their homes in several areas of the **Caucasus**, in **Tajikistan**, and, in the greatest numbers, in the former **Yugoslavia**, where up to 5 million people had been displaced by 1995. The opening of borders has also led to illegal flow of people from poorer areas, such as **Romania**, to central Europe, particularly **Germany**.

Of all European countries, Germany has had the most liberal laws on refugees, but the growing influx has caused domestic problems, including antiforeigner rioting in many cities. In 1993, Germany tightened its immigration rules.

RESTITUTIONS AND COMPENSATIONS are important components of the transformation of former Communist systems, particularly in **Eastern Europe**. These efforts to rectify damages caused by the previous regime have often led to new problems. What should be the cutoff date to consider returning confiscated property: When the Communists took over, in

During a summit meeting in May and June 1988, U.S. President Ronald Reagan and Soviet leader Mikhail Gorbachev made a historic stroll through Moscow's Red Square.

the late 1940s? Or just after the war? Or should one start with confiscations by Nazis? And how should victims of **Communism** and their descendants be compensated for loss of lives, terms in prison, and loss of jobs? How can monetary compensations be calculated? Will not the restitutions and compensations lead to new injustices?

ROMANI (GYPSIES) are one of the most visible European minorities. Thought to have perhaps originated in northern India, groups of wandering Gypsies came to Europe in the 14th century and spread throughout the continent. During World War II, Nazi **Germany** conducted a reign of terror against Gypsies, murdering about 500,000 of them in concentration camps.

It is not known how many Romani live in central and southern Europe, but the numbers certainly reach several million. Increasing criminality in the post-Communist period has often involved Romani, and this has in turn provoked right-wing attacks on them by **skinheads** and various neo-Nazi groups.

ROMANIA is a Balkan country on the Black Sea, slightly larger than Utah. Its 22.8 million people constitute the easternmost outpost of speakers of a Romance language: Romanian derives from Latin as it was spoken in the eastern part of the Roman Empire. Vlado Tepes the Impaler, a medieval Romanian hero who fought the Turks, was popularized in a 19th-century novel and ultimately transformed into the most famous of all Transylvanians, Count Dracula.

Long under the rule of foreign powers, present-day Romania began to emerge in the middle of the 19th century. Between the world wars, it was an absolute monarchy; in World War II, it fought on the side of Germans.

Unlike the rather peaceful government changes elsewhere in Eastern Europe, Romania's overthrow of Communism was accompanied by much death and destruction.

In 1944, the Communists took over and, for the next two decades, Romania closely followed the Soviet model.

A new period began in 1965, when **Nicolae Ceauşescu** was elevated to the leadership of Romania. The Ceauşescu era was first marked by an independent foreign policy and an opening to the West. In the 1980s, however, in order to reach his goal of paying off all foreign debt, Ceauşescu wreaked untold hardships upon the people. Drastic cuts in energy darkened Romanian streets, and in winter there was not enough heat. Food was exported and Romanians were half-starving. To compound the general bleakness of life, the government introduced the so-called "systematization plan," which called for the demolition of up to 7,000 villages and the transfer of their inhabitants into huge agro-industrial complexes.

The end of the Ceauşescu era was a combination of a popular revolt and a palace coup. Protests started on December 17, 1989, in the predominantly Hungarian city of Timişoara; on December 21, fighting broke out in the capital. Ceauşescu and his wife Elena fled, but they were captured and executed on December 25. The National Salvation Front (NSF), consisting mostly of former high Communist officials and led by **Ion Iliescu**, gained popular support by abolishing some of the most hated decrees of the dead dictator.

In May 1990, the first free Romanian elections since 1937 took place, with 82 registered political parties. The major ones, apart from the NSF, were poorly organized groups led by exiles. It was no surprise that the NSF won an overwhelming victory.

Ion Iliescu was reelected president in 1992, and the NSF remains in power. The government introduced a coupon **privatization** program in 1991, but it soon collapsed; subsequent economic reforms have been only halfhearted. Romania is no longer a dictatorship, but neither is it a fully democratic state with a free-market economy.

RUSSIA was the largest of the Soviet constituent republics, stretching from Eastern Europe to the Pacific. It is almost the same size as all of South America, and it has a population of 147.8 million. After the demise of the **U.S.S.R.** in December 1991, Russia became independent. **Boris Yeltsin** has been president of Russia since May 1990, when the Soviet Union still existed.

The origins of Russia go back to the tiny principality of Muscovy, which rose in the 12th century and gradually expanded its dominion over other duchies. Russia began to develop as a great power under Ivan the Terrible, the first czar (1533–84). Two other rulers, Peter the Great (1689–1725) and Catherine the Great (1762–96), tried to westernize Russia and bring it closer to Europe. From then on, Russia has had a complex relationship with Europe, emulating the European civilization and yet resisting Western ways. Meanwhile, the Russian territory grew and, in the 19th century, reached the Pacific. By the beginning of the 20th century, the Russian Empire had almost the same borders as its successor state, the U.S.S.R.

The new Russia, stripped of 14 surrounding republics, has painfully grappled with its loss of international prestige. Some newly independent regions, such as the **Baltic Republics** or Central Asian republics, were not central to the Russian self-identification, but **Ukraine**, **Belarus**, and most of the **Caucasus** have, since the early 19th century, been integral parts of the Russian national identity. Nicolai Gogol, for instance, one of the most famous "Russian" authors, was in fact a Belorussian, and Alexander Pushkin, the beloved "Russian" poet, lived and fought in the Caucasus.

More than 20 million ethnic Russians now live in the so-called "near abroad," the former Soviet republics that became independent nations in December 1991. Russia has been using the **Commonwealth of Independent States** as one of the vehicles by which to reestablish its economic and military ties with these republics.

The time since independence has been one of the most wrenching periods in all of Russian history. Still, amid the declining living standards, lost illusions, disruption of the old rules of the game, rising criminality, and widespread corruption, there nonetheless remain many reasons for hope.

Within three short years, Russia has managed to privatize half of its economy; it is still in bad shape, but with prospects for improvement and stabilization in 1996. The political transformation has not been smooth; major conflicts included a bloody contest between president **Boris Yeltsin** and parliament in October 1993, and a mishandled military operation in **Chechnya** in early 1995. Yet Russia has also developed some basic democratic institutions and practices, such as the Constitutional Court and trial by jury. Some optimists even believe that the former Communist giant could become a relatively prosperous free-market society in less than two decades.

SAKHAROV, ANDREI (1921–89), the father of the Soviet H-bomb, became, in 1953, the youngest member of the Soviet Academy of Sciences. In the early 1960s, he began to challenge Soviet authorities, and his human-rights activities earned him the Nobel Peace Prize in 1975.

After Sakharov sharply criticized the Soviet invasion of Afghanistan in December 1979, he was exiled to the town of Gorky. One day in

September 1986, a telephone was suddenly installed in his apartment, and the next day a personal call from **Mikhail Gorbachev** summoned the exiled **dissident** to Moscow. It was an event without precedent in Soviet history. In April 1989, Sakharov was elected to the Congress of People's Deputies, but he died of a heart attack the following December.

SARAJEVO, the capital of **Bosnia and Herzegovina**, has come to personify the cruelty of ethnic strife that has afflicted so much of the post-Communist world. Besieged by Serbian guerrilla forces in the surrounding hills, the city that had become known worldwide during the Winter Olympic Games in 1984 was bombarded and fired upon for almost four years, with few interruptions.

Sarajevo, the capital of Bosnia and Herzegovina, underwent four years of nearly constant bombardment by Serbian forces. Thousands of people died or became refugees.

SERBIA was the largest of the six republics comprising the pre-1992 **Yugoslavia**. Serbs are a Slavic people who are predominantly Orthodox Christians; their language is written in the Cyrillic script. In the early Middle Ages, Serbs had their own kingdom. Then, in 1389, they were defeated by the Turks at the Battle of Kosovo, which they still remember as a crucial moment of their history. They remained under Ottoman rule for centuries.

In 1987, when hard-line nationalist **Slobodan Milošević** became the leader of the Serbian Communist Party, Serbia set out on a path of ethnic conflict with the other nationalities of Yugoslavia. The first clashes—in the province of **Kosovo**, inhabited mostly by Albanians—were vastly overshadowed at first by brutal fighting in **Croatia** in 1991, and an even more brutal and much longer war in **Bosnia and Herzegovina** from 1992 to 1995. Prevailing world opinion considers the Serbs the chief aggressors in the ethnic wars; the Serbs tend to see themselves as victims.

SHEVARDNADZE, EDUARD (1928–), a native of **Georgia**, became known throughout the world as **Mikhail Gorbachev**'s foreign minister from 1985 to 1990. In March 1992, Shevardnadze returned to his native country and became chairman of Georgia's provisional State Council. In October 1992, he was elected by 90 percent of the voters to the post of speaker of the parliament. Widely respected for his efforts to bring peace to Georgia, he was elected to the presidency in August 1995.

"SHOOT-TO-KILL" was a policy of the government of **East Germany**, which ordered border guards to kill anyone trying to cross into West **Germany**. According to 1992 estimates, more than 200 East Germans were killed in such attempts. **Erich Honecker** and other former East German officials were charged with manslaughter in connection with this policy, but only several border guards were actually sentenced to prison terms.

SKINHEADS are young men (and sometimes women), usually less than 20 years old, often poorly educated, and frequently unemployed, who hold racist political views aimed particularly against **Romani** and other people with darker skin; the term "skinhead" derives from their often shaved heads. Skinhead groups can be found in many post-Communist countries, particularly in Central Europe. They are close to neo-Nazi organizations and have been responsible for much violence.

East Germany carried out a "shoot-to-kill" policy on any person trying to escape into West Germany. More than 200 people were killed while trying to flee to the West.

SLOVAKIA was the eastern half of **Czechoslovakia**; since January 1993, it has been an independent country about the size of New Hampshire and Vermont combined. Its mostly mountainous territory is inhabited by 5.3 million people. For 1,000 years, Slovakia was part of **Hungary**. Its only period of political independence before 1993 came during World War II, when it became a puppet Nazi state. After the war, it again became part of Czechoslovakia.

The Slovak yearning for an independent national identity became personified in populist politician **Vladimír Mečiar**, who during 1991 and 1992 got into a deepening conflict with Czech politicians. The sover-

On January 31, 1993, Slovakia became an independent nation, an event accompanied by much celebration. Since then, the Slovak government has become increasingly authoritarian.

eignty declaration by the Slovak National Council in July 1992 proclaimed that "the thousand years' striving of the Slovak nation for self-realization has been accomplished." Slovakia became an independent country on January 1, 1993.

The first three years of independence have not led to a disastrous economic collapse, as many had predicted, although political developments have illustrated just how different Slovakia is from the **Czech Republic**. The increasingly authoritarian methods of Mečiar's government led in late 1995 to protest notes from the **United States** and the **European Union**, which criticized the governing party's efforts to drive the opposition out of parliament and the mounting campaign against Slovakia's president, Michal Kováč.

SLOVENIA, one of the six constituent republics of pre-1992 **Yugoslavia** and, since June 1991, an independent country, lies in the northern part of the Balkan Peninsula, bordering on Austria. The New Jersey-sized nation has a population of about 2 million.

Slovenia was the richest and the most Westernized of all the Yugoslav republics, factors which helped smooth its post-Communist developments. Although **privatization** has been much slower than in such countries as the **Czech Republic**, **Poland**, and **Hungary**, the economy is doing well and growing. The present leadership consists mostly of the former Communists who led Slovenia when it was still part of Yugoslavia.

SNEGUR, MIRCEA, a former Communist turned nationalist, was elected president of the Soviet republic of **Moldova** in December 1991 and re-elected in February 1994. Snegur has proved to be one of the more capable of post-Communist leaders, quickly leading his country through a major economic transformation.

SOCIALISM, a word that dates from the early 19th century, has been one of the most abused and misused political terms of the 20th century. It has had many meanings: when **Stalin** built his "socialism in one country," the system he had in mind was a society totally controlled by him, with much emphasis on heavy industry, forced labor, and merciless struggle against the "class enemy." **Alexander Dubček**'s "socialism with a human face" was a more benevolent system, in which the Communist Party would still rule, but in consultation with other groups in the society. Yet another kind is the socialism of western social democratic parties, which advocate the modern "welfare state."

SOLIDARITY, an independent trade union in **Poland**, was the major protagonist in the last decade of Eastern European **Communism**. On August 14, 1981, an unemployed electrician named **Lech Wałęsa** began to lead a 17-day occupation strike in the shipbuilding city of Gdansk that resulted in the formation of the Solidarity trade union. The union soon claimed a membership of 10 million. During the next 15 months, it rapidly evolved into a powerful organization that began to demand free elections and a referendum on forming a legitimate non-Communist government. On December 13, 1981, under pressure from the **U.S.S.R.**, Polish prime minister **Wojciech Jaruzelski** declared martial law, suspended Solidarity, and arrested its leaders and activists—more than 10,000 people altogether.

But this was just one lost battle. With the absence of Soviet pressure after **Mikhail Gorbachev** came to power, Solidarity reasserted itself. In 1989, it regained a legal status and participated in the partially free elections for the Polish parliament, winning virtually all available seats.

In the initial euphoria following the overthrow of Communism in the former Soviet Union, countless statues of Communist heroes were toppled and otherwise desecrated.

Once the Communist adversary was gone, Solidarity split and in 1990 divided into two broad factions: the right-leaning Center Agreement, led by Wałęsa; and the left-leaning Citizens' Movement for Democratic Action, associated with urban intellectuals. By 1995, Solidarity had lost most of its influence.

In 1981, the independent trade union Solidarity emerged in the shipbuilding city of Gdansk, Poland. In a matter of months, Solidarity had a membership of over 10 million.

SOLZHENITSYN, ALEKSANDR (1918–), a leading Soviet **dissident** and a winner of the Nobel Prize for Literature in 1970. He was forcibly exiled from the **U.S.S.R.** in early 1974 after he published his *Gulag Archipelago*, considered one of the most important books of the 20th century for its vivid revelation of the horrors of the system of prisons and forced labor camps established under **Stalin**.

Solzhenitsyn settled in Vermont and concentrated on writing his mammoth reevaluation of Soviet history. His Soviet citizenship was restored in August 1990 and, in May 1994, he returned to **Russia**. His regular TV talk program was cancelled in September 1995; among the reasons given for the cancellation was that he never seemed to listen to what others said and that he was "unremittingly gloomy."

STALIN, JOSEPH (1879–1953), was for a quarter century the supreme Soviet leader. He made the **U.S.S.R.** a world superpower and he greatly contributed to the defeat of Hitler during World War II, but at the same time, he inflicted extreme suffering on his entire country. No one killed as many Communists as he did; indeed, during the height of his reign of terror, in the 1930s, it was much safer for a Communist to live in a Western country than in the Soviet Union.

Joseph Stalin (left, in 1945 with U.S. President Harry Truman and British Prime Minister Winston Churchill) gave Soviet Communism much of its authoritarian nature.

Stalin, although Georgian by birth, was a product of Russian history. The system created by him caused so much damage not only because it was brutal and intolerant, but also because it systematically rewarded the worst human qualities—subservience, dishonesty, lack of initiative, servility, and envy—and punished such qualities as courage, creativity, industriousness, and truthfulness.

More devious than Hitler, Stalin duped quite a number of Westerners, who praised him for his simplicity and charm. The **personality cult** elevated him to a godlike position. Despite several decades of **de-Stalinization**, it was only in the late 1980s that the Soviet people learned that their beloved leader was perhaps the greatest criminal in human history, responsible for 30 million to 50 million deaths.

TAJIKISTAN, a Central Asian republic about the size of Wisconsin, has 5.9 million people; until 1991, it was part of the **U.S.S.R.** Tajikistan is a mountainous country known for its sheepherding; it also has the world's largest deposits of silver. The Tajiks are a Persian-speaking people; even during the Soviet era, they lived in very traditional ways.

From August 1991 until early 1993, Tajikistan was a battleground, with Communist and opposition forces (the latter consisting of anti-Communists and Islamic fundamentalists) repeatedly locked in armed conflict. This civil war claimed more than 2,000 casualties. After a brief period when a non-Communist government was in power in late 1992, a pro-Russian government has been in charge, supported by about 20,000 Russian troops.

TER-PETROSYAN, LEVON (1945–), president of **Armenia** since 1990. There were large rallies against him in early 1993, when he was blamed for the economic policies, the energy crisis, and his handling of the

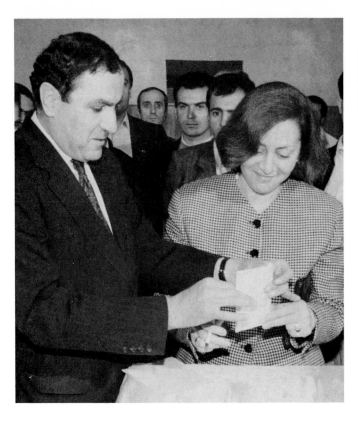

Levon Ter-Petrosyan (left, with his wife Ludmila) has managed to hold onto the presidency of Armenia despite setbacks in the war with Azerbaijan. His economic policies have garnered much praise from the United States and Western Europe.

Nagorny Karabakh conflict. Despite this criticism, he has firmly led the country and won praise from Western economists for making Armenia "a model of economic self-discipline."

TITO, JOSIP BROZ (1892– 1980), born in **Croatia**, was the powerful postwar leader of **Yugoslavia**. He led the Communist guerrillas during World War II, and then remained the paramount chief of the country until his death. Although Tito was an authoritarian ruler, he was not a cruel dictator like **Stalin** or **Ceauşescu**. He held the country together, balancing age-old ethnic animosities and turning Yugoslavia into a showcase of a relatively liberal Communist country.

TUDJMAN, FRANJO (1922–), president of **Croatia** since 1990, and head of the right-of-center Croatian Democratic Union. His nationalist bent—although evident from early on—has been overshadowed by the rhetoric of **Serbia**'s **Slobodan Milošević**. Tudjman led the Croatian army in two successful offensives in 1995, regaining the Bosnian-held territories of Croatia. Apparently modeling himself on **Tito** (under whom he served just after World War II as the youngest general in the Yugoslav army), he has begun to wear flashy uniforms and likes to be called "Father of the Nation."

Franjo Tudjman has been the president of Croatia since 1990. His recapture of Croatian territory held by the Serbs has greatly raised his stature among the citizens of his country.

TURKMENISTAN is an independent Central Asian republic about the size of Nevada and Utah combined, with 4.1 million inhabitants. It has the fourth-largest reserves of natural gas in the world. Turkmenistan is a one-party state; elections in December 1994 were like old Soviet elections: all candidates for the parliamentary seats were unopposed. President Saparmurat Niyazov had his term of office extended until 1999 in a referendum held in February 1994, in which all but 212 citizens of the country voted "yes."

UKRAINE was the second-largest constituent republic of the **U.S.S.R.**; it is twice the size of Arizona and has 51.5 million people. Centering around the ancient city of Kiev, Ukrainians have had a love-hate relationship with Russians for centuries. They often disputed **Russia**'s claim to continuity with the Kievan Rus, which arose in the 10th century. Prince Vladimir of Kiev accepted Christianity in 998.

Ukraine became independent in late 1991. One of the first problems the country had to grapple with—apart from an economic crisis—was the control of the Black Sea naval fleet stationed in Sevastopol, a port in the **Crimea**. Ukraine was also reluctant to give up the nuclear weapons in its possession, but finally signed an agreement in early 1994 to scrap them.

Under President Leonid Kravchuk, a Communist turned nationalist, the economy collapsed; in 1994 some foreign observers even considered Ukraine a "dying" country. Then an unexpected turnaround happened: Leonid Kuchma was elected president in July 1994. Campaigning on a platform of gradual rapprochement with Russia, Kuchma surprised everyone by turning instead to the West, introducing a thorough **price liberalization**, stabilizing the currency, and initiating **privatization** in early 1995. He also managed to get Western credits; six months after being elected, his approval rating stood at 58 percent.

UNION OF SOVIET SOCIALIST REPUBLICS (the **U.S.S.R.** or the Soviet Union), was for most of the 20th century the largest country in the world. Almost 2.5 times the size of the **United States**, it stretched from central Europe to the Pacific across 11 time zones; it had more than 100 nationalities and 112 officially recognized languages. A country of contrasts, its social and political settings ranged from **Estonia**, a Westernized Baltic country, to the Chukchi Siberian groups in the northeast whose lives resemble those of the Canadian Eskimo, and to the Muslim republics in Central Asia.

The Soviet Union was the heir to the Russian Empire. When the Bolsheviks seized power in 1917 in the **October Revolution**, and emerged victorious after three years of civil war, they believed that they started a "world revolution." Instead, their social experiment became one of the two greatest tragedies, together with Nazism, of the 20th century.

The Soviet Union went through several periods: the early revolutionary euphoria, **Stalin**'s terror of the 1930s, a great patriotic upsurge during World War II, and then the postwar period of empire building. **Khrushchev**'s "**de-Stalinization**" and **Brezhnev**'s **détente** followed, and finally came the period of "stagnation" in the 1980s. By then, it was becoming obvious that the system did not work. The Soviet Union was a world superpower with a great arsenal of nuclear weapons and space technology, and yet the average villagers lived almost the same way as

they did in the 19th century. In the cities, the time spent standing in lines for everyday items represented millions of lost hours of work and instilled the people with an overwhelming resentment and dissatisfaction. Nothing seemed to work, and no one seemed to believe in anything anymore; the teachings of **Marxism-Leninism** were just empty formulas repeated automatically when required. Alcoholism became a major problem as both men and women resorted to the ubiquitous Russian vodka to drown their sorrows.

When **Mikhail Gorbachev** started his reforms in 1985, he opened a Pandora's box. His policies of *glasnost* and *perestroika* shook the stagnant waters of the system, and at first promised to be the miraculous medicine needed to put the society back into shape. It turned out, however, that the patient was even sicker than was apparent, and while Gorbachev was reaping applause throughout the Western world, his country was getting into ever deeper difficulties: growing economic problems, shortages of everything, ethnic conflicts, separatism, and loss of political authority.

By the end of 1990, a mood of national exasperation had taken hold of the country. Gorbachev responded by first allying himself with hard-liners, which prompted the resignation of **Eduard Shevardnadze** in December and led to the violent crackdown in the **Baltic Republics** in January 1991. In April 1991, Gorbachev changed his mind and concluded an agreement with nine Soviet leaders about a new union treaty intended to give individual republics much greater independence from Moscow. This, in turn, provoked fear in the Communist "old guard" and culminated in the botched coup of August 1991. After that, the fate of the

Soviet Union was sealed: four more months of political and social upheaval ended with the final demise of the Communist colossus on December 25, 1991.

UNITED STATES appeared on the European political scene briefly at the end of World War I and for several subsequent years, and then retreated back across the Atlantic. It was not even a member of the precursor of the United Nations, the League of Nations. Since World War II, however, the United States has been a crucial player in European politics. Its doctrine of the "containment of **Communism**" was a bulwark against Soviet expansionism.

Citizens of Communist countries were fascinated by the United States, the archenemy of their governments. Despite continuous hostile propaganda, America was admired as a country of jeans, rock and roll, and tall, smiling people with beautiful white teeth. Generations of central European children still continue to read adventure books by Karl May, a 19th-century German author who never set foot in America but nonetheless wrote a series of novels about American Indians. The United States was also known from movies and from the works of such popular writers as Ernest Hemingway and Kurt Vonnegut.

Since 1989, the United States has lost some of its magic for people in the former Communist countries, thanks both to mushrooming transatlantic trips and a massive penetration of such American staples as McDonald's, TV sitcoms, and B movies. Yet it still remains an attractive, formidable country. The U.S. part in seeking to end the war in **Bosnia and Herzegovina** has shown its continuing role in European politics.

UZBEKISTAN, twice as large as Utah, is a Central Asian republic with about 22.1 million inhabitants. The country has a colorful history: in the 14th century, the city of Samarkand was the capital of the sophisticated empire of Timurlane. Uzbekistan became part of the Russian Empire in the early 19th century. Today, Uzbekistan is the only Central Asian country that has no Russian troops on its soil.

Uzbekistan's president, **Islam Karimov**, and other officials in power are former Communists. Opposition groups and leaders have been persecuted and have virtually disappeared without much protest from the citizenry, most of whom say that they prefer a strong, stable government. Thanks to its rich mineral deposits, including the world's largest gold mine, the country had become almost self-sufficient in basic commodities by 1995.

VUKOVAR, a city in easternmost **Croatia**, became a ghost town in late 1991 when it was almost totally demolished in the war between Croats and Serbs. Most of its 45,000 inhabitants were either killed or fled.

WAŁĘSA, LECH (1943–), an electrician with only a high-school education, was the leader of **Solidarity** in 1980–81, and the Nobel Peace Prize winner in 1983. His political activism began during the December 1970 strikes in Gdansk; by August 1980, he had become an international celebrity. In 1987, he published his autobiography, *A Way of Hope*. On December 9, 1990, Wałęsa, in a landslide victory, was elected president of **Poland**, but because of continuing economic problems and political instability, his popularity gradually dissipated. He lost to a former Communist in the November 1995 presidential elections.

WARSAW PACT was the name of a military alliance formed in 1955 in response to **NATO**. Its original members were **Albania**, **Bulgaria**, **Czechoslovakia**, **East Germany**, **Hungary**, **Poland**, **Romania**, and the **U.S.S.R.** Albania stopped participating in the early 1960s. The only military action that the Warsaw Pact armies ever took was the invasion of Czechoslovakia in August 1968. The alliance was formally dissolved in July 1991.

In August 1991, Boris Yeltsin led the opposition to an attempted coup by Soviet hard-liners. As Russia's president, Yeltsin has had to deal with the dismantling of the vast Communist system.

YELTSIN, BORIS (1931–), president of **Russia** since 1990, is the foremost leader in the post-Communist world. His career in the late 1980s provided vivid proof of the depth of changes in the **U.S.S.R.** In the fall of 1987, Yeltsin was attacked by **Mikhail Gorbachev** and sacked from the Moscow municipal committee. If **Stalin** had taken a dislike to him, he would have paid with his life; under **Brezhnev**, he would have become a "non-person" (like **Khrushchev**). Instead, Yeltsin made a comeback in 1989, when he was elected to the Congress of People's Deputies.

In June 1990, Yeltsin was elected president of Russia; the following month, at the 28th Party Congress, he quit the Communist Party. By the fall of 1990, Yeltsin had become vastly more popular than Gorbachev, and in August 1991, he led the opposition to the attempted coup by Soviet hard-liners.

Gradually, his popularity went down, as the economic and political situation continued to worsen. Like his predecessor, he tried to balance between reformers and conservatives, but since late 1993 he has had to bow to the latter, particularly in international and territorial matters. His approval rating in early 1995 was just 14 percent, and he further lost his moral stature after the Russian invasion of **Chechnya**. His political difficulties have been compounded by health problems; there have also been persistent rumors about his alcoholism. After eight years of struggle he seemed quite exhausted in late 1995, but he was still intending to stand for presidential elections in June 1996.

YUGOSLAVIA is now a name for two political entities. From 1929 until 1992, with an interruption during World War II, it described the federation of six republics, **Serbia**, **Croatia**, **Slovenia**, **Bosnia and Herzegovina**, **Macedonia**, and Montenegro. This mosaic burst apart in the early 1990s. In April 1992, a new, truncated Yugoslavia was proclaimed, consisting only of Serbia and Montenegro. It is about half the size of the previous Yugoslavia and has 10.5 million inhabitants.

During World War II, Yugoslavia was the scene of a fierce guerrilla war between partisans and groups allied with the Fascists; some 1.7 million Yugoslavs were killed. The fighting left deep scars and lingering animosities, especially between the Serbs and the Croats. After the war, the charismatic Communist leader **Josip Broz Tito** held the country firmly together until his death in 1980. Under Tito, Yugoslavia balanced on a dividing line between a typical Communist state (it had only one party, with supreme powers; there was press censorship; and people were put in prison for political reasons) and a relatively liberal society (travel abroad was much easier than elsewhere in the Communist world; the political suppression was much milder).

When Tito died, the buried nationalist passions reemerged, fanned by the president of Serbia, **Slobodan Milošević**, and his dream of creating a "Greater Serbia." Serbs in Croatia and later in Bosnia and Herzegovina took to arms, and friendly Yugoslavia turned into a nightmare. In September 1992, Yugoslavia was expelled from the United Nations—the first time any sitting member was ejected.

By late 1994, Milošević began to be interested in ending the conflict. This change and the military upsets in the summer and early fall of 1995 finally led to a negotiated peace settlement that was signed in November 1995. On November 23, the United Nations lifted the embargo on Yugoslavia that had been imposed in May 1992.

ZHELEV, ZHELYU (1935–), the president of **Bulgaria** since August 1990, was one of the very few Bulgarian **dissidents** during the Communist era. In 1965, he was expelled from the Communist Party because he had questioned the basis of Lenin's philosophical theories in an essay. Zhelev won reelection to a second presidential term in January 1992. He is very popular and remains a force for stability and democracy.

ZHIVKOV, TODOR (1911–), the leader of the Communist Party in **Bulgaria** from 1954 until his removal in November 1989, had the second-longest tenure among East European leaders, after the Albanian Enver Hoxha. In September 1992, Zhivkov was convicted of embezzling state funds and sentenced to seven years in prison. He was the first Communist leader to be tried in an open trial.

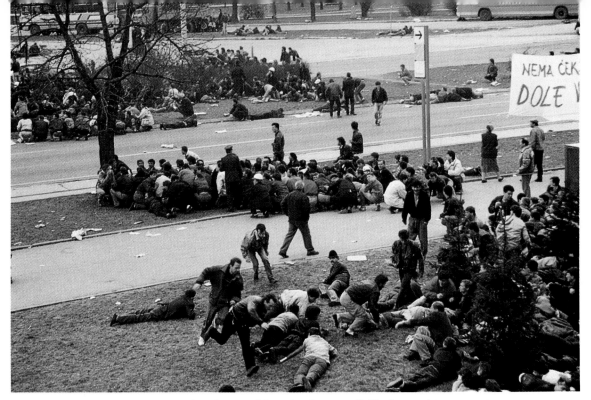

Ethnic unrest has swept through many of the regions long controlled by Communist governments.

Looking Toward the Next Century

Communist regimes in Europe and in the Soviet Union were toppled with surprising ease. In the wake of this massive social transformation, millions of people from Berlin to Tashkent have had to cope with radical changes. The tremendous difficulties brought about by the disintegration of Communism and its complex structures are far from over.

Post-Communist Challenges

Ethnic violence. At the end of 1995, it seemed as though much of the post-Communist violence had wound down. People in Bosnia and Herzegovina were no longer hearing the sound of shelling mortars or falling bombs; instead, they warily observe the arriving multinational force that will oversee the implementation of the peace agreement. In Tajikistan and in the Caucasus, the fighting has largely subsided as well. There is no guarantee that violence will not flare up again, but the prospects for the immediate future looked better in late 1995 than they have for the previous several years. The external scars of the wars—destroyed buildings, roads, and bridges—will, of course, be easier to fix than will the psychological wounds.

Building democracy. Democratic institutions and practices have already developed in those countries that had some historical experience with democracy. But even without a democratic legacy, the post-Communist republics have by and large discarded their more-onerous totalitarian features. There is still much work to do: educate young people for democracy; train new leaders; set up functioning, independent judicial systems; and establish regional and local administrations.

Young people in the former Communist world are no longer afraid. Increased personal and professional contacts with Western democracies will continue to play a key role by fostering political freedoms and helping to cultivate the art of civilized political discourse and compromise.

Economic transformation. Pessimists point to a number of disappointments that have accompanied the post-Communist transformation: widespread corruption; the continuing role of former Communist bosses in the economic sphere; the plight of pensioners who have seen their living standards go down; and the recklessness of the new entrepreneurial class. There is another side to the coin, however: in almost all of the formerly Communist countries, important steps have been taken toward free-market economies. Individual entrepreneurship is now permitted, and prices have been liberalized. In many countries, the process of privatizing state enterprises has begun; some countries have created stock markets, and many have attracted foreign investments.

Differences are mostly due to historical tradition: the small republic of Slovenia, for instance, is now, economically, on a par with Portugal; Belarus, by contrast, has undergone virtually no economic transformation. Interestingly, the authoritarian governments of the Central Asian republics—countries with no history of modern capitalism—have begun to introduce private ownership of land and to support individual entrepreneurship.

Even the most economically advanced of the formerly Communist countries will have to fine-tune their financial systems, adopt legislation on such matters as bankruptcies (something unheard of in the Communist past) and foreign investment, and set clear rules on various economic undertakings. Obsolete industrial plants will need to close down and new technologies will have to be introduced. A major problem is the communication infrastructure, which desperately needs fixing everywhere.

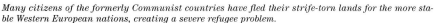

Many citizens of the formerly Communist countries have fled their strife-torn lands for the more stable Western European nations, creating a severe refugee problem.

Long-suppressed bigotries quickly resurfaced in the newly liberalized Eastern European societies. In some places, groups of neo-Nazis and skinheads have terrorized the immigrant population.

Criminality and racial violence. The disappearance of rigid controls has led to a rise in criminal behavior throughout what was once the Communist world. Street crime has increased dramatically, and organized crime has mushroomed, with gangs dealing drugs, smuggling refugees, and engaging in various swindling schemes, robberies, and murders. Contract killings, once seen only in American gangster movies, have become commonplace in Russia, and even occur in such orderly countries as the Czech Republic. With the unprecedented transfer of property in recent years, corruption has reached unparalleled levels. The struggle against criminality needs to intensify.

The fall of Communism has also led to hundreds of incidents of racial hatred. Many of them have occurred in the former East Germany, where groups of young skinheads and neo-Nazis have attacked housing complexes inhabited by immigrants. In Central Europe, similar violent groups terrorize Romani (Gypsies), Vietnamese, and other dark-skinned individuals. These young thuds are often unemployed and blame the refugees for their difficulties. Racial violence has even spread to liberal Scandinavia. Only a concerted effort from all European countries will overcome this problem.

The environment. Many places in the former Communist world are ecological disasters. For years, people knew that they lived in unhealthy conditions; unfortunately, the truth about the ecological damage proved to be even harsher than many suspected. In contrast to the West, where ecological concerns began to play a role in the late 1960s, the Communist world waited three more decades before recognizing that it had a problem—three decades in which the environment was further abused. These matters are now openly discussed, but openness is not enough: vast amounts of money are needed to reverse the damage—money that is in very short supply. Some improvements have taken place: rivers in central Europe are a little cleaner, and a return to private farming and forestry has in some cases been beneficial to nature. Still, at least several decades are needed before the former Communist countries can compare in environmental protection with Western Europe and the United States.

Social and cultural change. This is the most difficult challenge of all, compounded by the general anxieties and uncertainties of the post-modernist era with its instantaneous worldwide communication. In a sense, the former Communist countries are now jumping from the 19th century into the 21st, skipping the decades of social and cultural evolution that occurred in Western Europe and the United States. Dozens of issues have been opened to discussion: How important is material progress and wealth? How should Western civilization deal with non-Western societies? What should the role of women be? Many people who were among the staunchest opponents of Communism now criticize the consumer style of living, the obsession with careers, and the diminishing role of culture.

Another ongoing change has to do with how people in Communist countries came to rely on the state to take care of many of their needs. These people must now learn to be more individually responsible for their lives.

Facing the past. Victims of Communism remain largely unsatisfied. Very few of the former leaders and bosses have been put on trial, and most of those responsible for the Communist oppression are free and prospering. Many of the younger ones have even become unscrupulous capitalists. Attempts at an open exploration of the past are complicated by the simple fact that former or current members of the Communist Party are now in power in almost all countries. Perhaps a certain period of time must pass before a balanced reevaluation can be made.

Regional Outlook

Central Europe. This is where the most progress has been made. Poland, the Czech Republic, and Hungary are in the forefront of both economic and political changes, and will be the first of the former Communist countries to fully join the West. Slovakia is trailing behind, mostly because of its brash prime Minister Vladimír Mečiar. Slovenia, the

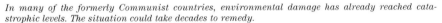

In many of the formerly Communist countries, environmental damage has already reached catastrophic levels. The situation could take decades to remedy.

Many people in formerly Communist countries have had trouble adjusting to the loss of the Communist "safety net." In recent years, former Communists have won many elections.

northernmost republic of former Yugoslavia, can also be considered part of Central Europe; it is doing very well indeed.

Former Yugoslavia. The Joint Endeavor multinational force will oversee the implementation of the peace settlement and the elections, which are to take place in mid-1996. The mission will prove to be a dangerous one. Some Bosnian Serbs, particularly those indicted by the International Tribunal at The Hague as war criminals, are likely to pursue their war. The fiercest fighters on the Muslim side have been volunteers from such countries as Afghanistan, Iran, and Libya; they are supposed to leave the country, but some of them will probably remain. The Dayton agreement also says that refugees are to return to their homes, but how that will work in practice remains unsettled. The physical rebuilding of Bosnia and Herzegovina constitutes another major task.

With the lifting of the embargo, the economy of the truncated new Yugoslavia (consisting of Serbia and Montenegro) could quickly revive. The country will also need an open discussion about the war and about Serbian atrocities, mostly against Muslims, but this will require considerable courage and time.

President Tudjman of Croatia will likely remain popular for his efforts to end the war. Nonetheless, he will have to take into account the 55 percent of the voters who did not support his party in the 1995 elections.

The media do not frequently report on Macedonia. Once the country solves its dispute with Greece, its major obstacle to peaceful development will be removed.

The Balkans. Albania, Romania, and Bulgaria lag behind the Central European countries. Economic transformation is very slow, and the general political culture continues to bear multiple traces of its authoritarian past. All these countries are, nonetheless, eager to attract Western investment; they will therefore have to implement both political and economic reforms.

Baltic Republics. These three tiny nations won the world's sympathy when they stood up like little Davids defying the Russian Goliath. Since those heady days, the mood has sobered as they grapple with economic reforms and continuing dependence on Russia. Estonia has the brightest outlook, thanks to its Scandinavian links.

Russia. The Soviet Union's successor state remains a formidable uncertainty, even though some Western observers had begun to sound optimistic in 1995. The outcome of presidential elections in 1996 will set the course for years to come; no one expects Russia to return to its totalitarian past. Despite tremendous problems, Russians have learned within six short years to expect that their governments will be chosen in open, real elections, and they have started to take the freedom to express their views for granted. Almost one-fifth of the population, the younger generation, supports both the economic and political changes, but older Russians continue to remember the good old Communist days of "law and order." One major problem of Russia: how to maintain its status as a great world power.

Belarus, Ukraine, and Moldova. Belarus, which never really wanted independence, has been eager to reestablish as many ties with Russia as possible. Ukraine, on the other hand, has surprised everyone by increasingly turning to the West—even though its president, Leonid Kuchma, who was mainly responsible for this turn of events, campaigned on a platform of friendship with Russia. If the economic transformation goes well, Ukraine has the potential to become a strong East European country. Moldova is another qualified success: its leadership of former Communists is proving to be quite a capable management team.

The Caucasus. The fighting—between Armenia and Azerbaijan, between several minorities and the government in Georgia, and between the Russian government and Chechnyan rebels—has subsided. None of the contested issues is definitively solved, but all sides seem to be exhausted by the warring. Paradoxically, the three independent Caucasian republics might obtain more popular support for radical reforms precisely because of the violence: while elsewhere in the former Soviet Union, the economic pain of the transition has alienated much of the population, in Armenia, Azerbaijan, and Georgia people blame war for their problems. Now, with guns resting, they can—without nostalgia for the old Communist days—devote their energies to rebuilding.

Central Asia. In Tajikistan, there is no peace between Islamic fundamentalists and the pro-Moscow Communist government, although at the end of 1995, a full-blown armed conflict seemed unlikely. The largely authoritarian Central Asian republics are trying to transform their economies and increase their autonomy, although they will nonetheless remain in Russia's sphere of influence for years to come.

Unless a cataclysmic event takes place in Russia, small incremental improvements will likely continue throughout much of formerly Soviet-dominated world. The European Union will admit several new members around the year 2000 and will hopefully work out some mutually beneficial and acceptable arrangement with Russia. One unresolved question is the future of NATO. Central European countries would like to join it as soon as possible, but Russia is strongly opposed. It might be mostly rhetoric, as the recent developments in Bosnia and Herzegovina have shown: in the operation Joint Endeavor, led by NATO, several thousand Russian soldiers are taking part. Hardly anyone could have foreseen this even five years ago.

INDEX

ILLUSTRATION CREDITS

The following list acknowledges, according to page, the sources of illustrations used in LANDS AND PEOPLES SPECIAL EDITION: THE CHANGING FACE OF EUROPE. The credits are listed illustration by illustration—top to bottom, left to right. When the name of the photographer has been listed with the source, the two are separated by a slash. If two or more illustrations appear on the same page, their credits are separated by semicolons.

2   © Francis Apesteguy/Gamma-Liaison
3   AP/Wide World Photos
4   © Peter Turnley/Black Star
7   © Keystone
8   © Christian Valdes/Lehtikuva Oy/Saba
10 © Jose Nicolas/Sipa Press
11 © Thierry Chesnot/Sipa Press
13 © William Stevens/Gamma-Liaison
14 © Tania Makeeva/Sipa Press
15 AP/Wide World Photos
17 © J. Jones/Sygma
19 © Terry Knerem/Sygma
21 © Patrick Chauvel/Sygma
23 © Bas Van Beek/Leo de Wys
24 © Thierry Orban/Sygma
26 © UPI/Bettmann; © Erich Lessing; © UPI/Bettmann
27 International News Photo
28 Paris Match; AP/Wide World Photos
29 © UPI/Bettmann
30 Both photos: © UPI/Bettmann
31 © Sygma; © UPI/Bettmann; © Keler/Sygma
32 © Roland Neveu/Gamma-Liaison; AP/Wide World Photos
33 © UPI/Bettmann; © Ed Wojtas; © David Burnett/Contact
34 AP/Wide World Photos
36 © Laski/Sipa Press; AP/Wide World Photos
37 © Kok/Gamma-Liaison
38 AP/Wide World Photos
40 © Yankelevitch/Sipa Press
41 © Sygma
43 © Shepard Sherbell/Saba; © D. Hudson/Sygma
44 © Witt/Sipa Press
45 © Luc Delahaye/Sipa Press; AP/Wide World Photos
47 © A. Nogues/Sygma
48 © Alexandra Avakian/Woodfin Camp & Assoc.
49 © Frederic Stevens/Sipa Press
50 © J. Langevin/Sygma
51 © Chip Hires/Gamma-Liaison; © Wojteck Laski/Sipa Press
52 © Chris Niedenthal/Black Star
53 © Luc Delahaye/Sipa Press; © Pocius/Sygma
54 © Roberto Koch/Saba; © Tilt Vermae/Lehtikuva/Saba; © Rudiger Schilight Stern/Black Star
55 © Jean-Claude Coutausse/Contact/Woodfin Camp & Assoc.; © Filip Horvat/Saba
56 © J. Langevin/Sygma; © Paul Miller/Black Star; © Reuters/Bettmann
57 © Reuters/Bettmann; © Paul Herve/Sipa Press
58 © East News/Sipa Press
59 © B. Markel/Gamma-Liaison; © Swersey/Gamma-Liaison
60 © Chip Hires/Gamma-Liaison; © A. Boulet/Sipa Press
61 © Gamma-Liaison; © Reuters/Bettmann
62 © Sergei Guneyev/Saba
63 © Andy Hernandez/Sipa Press; © Joshua Roberts/Sipa Press
64 © Diana Walker/Gamma-Liaison; © David Brauchli/Sygma; © Facelly/Sipa Press
65 © Alberto Pizzoli/Sygma; © E. Ortiz/Sygma
66 © Epix/Sygma; AP/Wide World Photos
67 © Shone/Gamma-Liaison; © Xinhua/Gamma-Liaison
68 © Sygma; © David Brauchli/Sygma
69 AP/Wide World Photos
70 AP/Wide World Photos
71 © Peter Turnley/Newsweek/Black Star
72 © J. Langevin/Sygma
74 © Laski/Sipa Press
75 © Matti Bjorkman/Saba
76 © Anthony Suau/Black Star
77 © Patrick Forestier
78 © B. Markel/Gamma-Liaison
79 © Steve Lehman/Saba
80 © Diana Walker/Gamma-Liaison; © V. Kiselyov/Lehtikuva/Woodfin Camp & Assoc.
83 © Frederico Mendes/Sipa Press
85 © Thierry Orban/Sygma
87 © Robert Wallis/Sipa Press
89 © A. Nogues/Sygma; © Chesnot/Sipa Press
90 © Shepard Sherbell/Saba
91 © Allan Tannenbaum/Sygma
92 © Francois Lehr/Sipa Press
93 © Thierry Orban/Sygma; © Jeremy Nicholl/Katz/Saba
94 © Pierre Adenis/Sipa Press
95 © Chesnot/Sipa Press
96 © Reuters/Bettmann
97 © T. Veermae/Lehtikuva/Saba
98 © Neal C. Lauron/Reuters/Archive Photos
99 © Sygma
101 AP/Wide World Photos
102 © Jurgen Vogt/The Image Bank
104 © A. Solomonov/RIA/Sipa Press
105 © Tass from Sovfoto
106 © Luc Delahaye/Sipa Press
108 © Francoise Demulder/Sipa Press
109 © UPI/Bettmann
110 © Van Cappellen/Rea/Saba
111 AP/Wide World Photos
112 © B. Bisson/Sygma
113 Signal Corps/Acme
114 © Reuters/Bettmann; © Filip Horvat/Saba
116 © P. Le Segretain/Sygma
118 © Peter Turnley/Black Star
120 © Demulder/Sipa Press
121 © Peter Turnley/Black Star
122 © R. Bossu/Sygma
123 © Dorigny/REA/Sygma
124 © Reuters/Bettmann

Cover and title page photo: © Steve Vidler/Leo de Wys
Contents page photos: © Peter Turnley/Black Star; © Steve Lehman/Saba; © David Brauchli/Sygma; © Peter Turnley/Black Star